How to live without FEAR & WORRY

K. Sri Dhammananda

BMS PUBLICATIONS
MALAYSIA

Publication of the
Buddhist Missionary Society,
123, Jalan Berhala,
Off Jalan Tun Sambanthan,
50470 Kuala Lumpur, Malaysia.

ISBN 967-9920-48-8

Typeset by:
Syarikat Broadway Typesetting Sdn. Bhd.,
Kuala Lumpur, Malaysia.

Reprinted for free distribution by
The Corporate Body of
the Buddha Educational Foundation
11F., 55 Hang Chow South Road Sec 1,
Taipei, Taiwan, R.O.C.

CONTENTS

PART II

HOW TO OVERCOME WORRY NOW

PART III

INGREDIENTS FOR HAPPINESS

PART IV

TECHNIQUES FOR HAPPY AND SUCCESSFUL LIVING

FOREWORD

'Men are born, they suffer, they die. That, according to Anatole France is how a wise man once summed up the human condition. On the other hand, some free thinkers say: 'Man is a little machine, made possible by an accidental arrangement of atoms and a naturalistic evolutionary process. Suffering is man's inescapable lot in his struggle for survival. It has no 'meaning' other than that, no purpose. Death is a dissolution of chemical elements; nothing else remains'.

While both the above are common observations amongst certain sceptics, materialists and even some great thinkers, other philosophers and religious teachers have tried to discover some meanings and purposes in life, especially with regard to the problem of suffering.

According to the Buddha, the characteristic of every component thing is that it appears, decays and disappears in a never-ending process. All component things are subject to ceaseless change and conflict (Dukkha). It is endured by all suffering beings who believe in a permanent entity or soul. This belief gives rise to selfish desire which can never be satisfied, thus leading to fear and worry.

The Buddha provided a moral base to his teachings when he declared that while there is suffering and uncertainty in existence, nevertheless it is possible for man to experience happiness both in its absolute as well as its temporal sense if he learns to distinguish between skilful and unskilful actions. To do this man must first have Right View which means that he must recognise the unsatisfactory nature of his existence and sensual pleasures and also to direct his life in the proper manner to see the end of uncertainty and un-satisfactoriness.

Why Worry

The first edition of **Why Worry** was published in 1967 (10,000 copies) and since then it has been in such great demand that it has been reprinted no less than six times at the rate of 5,000 copies per printing. Letters of appreciation and gratitude have poured in from various parts of the world – the U.S., U.K., Germany, South Africa and almost every Asian country. Those who have expressed their appreciation of the book are not only Buddhists but Hindus, Muslims, Christians and even some 'free thinkers'. The appeal of the book has been partly due to the fact that it has been written simply and without pretension and also because its main purpose was to reveal the facts of life not only from the Buddhist point of view but also by giving reasonable views from other religions and great thinkers. It was written primarily to provide comfort and solace to human beings in need of guidance to face the bewildering complexity of modern civilisation.

Some have even written in to say how they were prevented from committing suicide by reading the book, others to say that they read a few pages of it every night to help them to calm their minds to assure themselves that there are simple and practical solutions to the problems of the world.

Many things have happened since *Why Worry* first appeared; many changes have taken place. In the intervening years the author has gained new insights relating to human problems as a result of reading the numerous letters written to him as well as in his fruitful discussions with troubled people from all walks of life. It was decided that the publication of a new edition of the book would be most opportune at this time.

This expanded edition seeks to address itself to age-old problems and to those peculiar to our day and age. But its primary focus remains unchanged: that is, to show how one can live without fear and worry provided one has Right Understanding. It attempts to discuss problems from a practical and humanistic viewpoint. To this end, many quotations, anecdotes, witty sayings, fables and so on have been included to show how wise men have viewed the human condition across time and space. Many of these have an oriental flavour and some readers may have difficulty in relating to them and feel they are suitable only for those who belong to a particular culture. But such readers will benefit if they can differentiate between the setting of the stories and the point that is being made. After all, universal problems and truths apply equally well to all human beings.

It is fervently hoped that this book will give fresh inspiration and hope to whoever reads it without cynicism and doubt.

K. SRI DHAMMANANDA
WESAK DAY 19/05/89
B.E. 2533

Buddhist Vihara
123, Jalan Berhala
50470, Kuala Lumpur
Malaysia

ACKNOWLEDGEMENT

We wish to express our sincere thanks and appreciation to Messrs. Victor Wee and Vijaya Samarawickrama for assisting in editing the book and for their useful suggestions which helped to bring the book to its present form. We also like to thank Ms. Chong Hong Choo who had spent endless hours looking after innumerable details necessary in the production of the book, from its planning stage right up to its completion. Thanks are also due to Messrs. Charles Moreira, Lim Teong Chuan, L.L.G. Jayawardene, H.M.A. de Silva, Teh Thean Choo, Tan Teik Beng, Yau Yue Kai, Tan Siang Chye and Misses Lily See, Lim Mooi Hwa, Hema Cheah, Janet Teoh and Susie Lo for their assistance in one way or another, without which the present book would not have been possible.

PART I

WORRY AND ITS SOURCE

1

FEAR AND WORRY

We pay the price of fear and worry to live the life of a human being. Our susceptibility to anxiety is the root cause of our problems.

Fear and worry seem to be part and parcel of human life. One who is immersed in the mundane world is not free from these unpleasant mental states.

Why and what do people worry about? Their worries are due to various commitments and responsibilities they have. Their worries come in many various guises. They feel inadequate when they compare themselves with others. 'Maybe I'm not good enough to do that job' or 'I don't think I'm clever enough to make an impact.' They may be afraid to be themselves as they really are in the presence of others, so they end up saying to themselves: 'I can't let people get to know me as I really am. If I do so, they may lose confidence in me or belittle me.' So they act and pretend to be someone else when in fact they are not.

People worry a lot about their physical appearances. Men worry when they become bald headed, while women worry when wrinkles start to appear on their faces, or when they are too thin or too fat, too dark or too fair, too tall or too short and so on.

They are afraid of being criticised, attacked by others or censured by their superiors. They are afraid to present their ideas or opinions before a crowd for fear of being ridiculed, but feel angry with themselves whenever someone else presents the same idea and gets credit for it. They feel they are being hampered by criticisms, even when they know that such criticisms are undeserved and unjustified.

They are worried about their families. 'Maybe I'm not such a good father/mother/son/daughter after all.' Some husbands worry that their pretty young wives may go out with other men. At the same time some wives may worry that their handsome young husbands may leave them or spend their time with other girls. Unmarried people worry about how to get married while some married couples may worry about how lonely they are without children. On the other hand, those who have many children constantly worry about how best to bring them up; 'Maybe my wife/ husband no longer loves me and may desert me' or 'I wonder whether my children will take care of me in my old age.' Some parents worry unnecessarily over the safety of their children, having enough money for their daily household expenses, the security in their home, and the health of their loved ones.

In their workplace, they may have to face problems in carrying out assignments and have difficulties in making decisions. 'What if my decision proves to be wrong?' 'Should I sell my stocks and shares now or later?' 'Can my workers be trusted with money or will they cheat the company during my absence?' Some are worried about possible losses, of not getting a promotion or being entrusted with too many responsibilities. Some others worry thinking that their office mates are jealous of them.

In fact, the list of worries people face daily would be endless. Human existence is full of worries and fear which lurk within the dark inner corners of the mind. Man has so many fears – fear arising from insecurity, fear of enemies, fear of hunger, fear of sickness, fear of loss of wealth and possessions, fear of old age, fear of death and even fear of the next existence.

Not only does he worry and fear whenever things go wrong, he becomes worried even when things go on smoothly! He conjures a vague sense of fear in his mind that suddenly something may go wrong and that the happiness he now enjoys might turn to sorrow. Although some people say, no news means good news, people worry when there is no news. Such unfounded worries fill their life with undue fear. Such form of wretchedness befalls all mankind. And none are free from this except those who are perfect or pure in their minds.

The Cause of Worry

Of all adverse mental states, one of the most un-healthy and dangerous is prolonged worry. Why do people worry? In the ultimate analysis, there is only one answer. People worry because of the concept 'me' and 'mine', or what is known in Buddhism as the 'Delusion of Self'.

Nearly all animals lower than human beings are motivated by instinct. This is not so with man, who has superior thinking power as well as intuition. With his rational intellect, he creates the idea of a perma-nent ego for self preservation. Buddhism, is unique in the history of human thought in that it points out the Self-or-Soul idea is merely a concept, with no corres-pondence to reality. From this belief of self, a person develops wrong ideas of 'me' and 'mine', together with all cravings, selfish desires, conceit, pride and other unwholesome thoughts. This concept of 'self', is the main source of all problems, ranging from per-sonal conflicts to wars amongst nations.

From this idea of 'self', man believes in the false notion of a permanent body which must be satisfied and at times goes to extremes in satisfying the craving body. The fear of not having his needs and desires met to his full satisfaction brings him worry and anxiety.

Hence, worry is nothing more than a negative state of mind arising out of attachment to worldly pleasures. The stronger the attachment is to a thing, the greater is the fear of losing it. The moment one's particular need is satisfied a person starts longing for another.

In a similar way, one becomes afraid of getting or coming into contact with something considered undesirable. This attachment to pleasant feelings and dislike for the unpleasant ones gives rise to worry. Sometimes when taken to extremes, fear may arise because of attachment or association with specific objects or situations which are harmless in themselves. Such cases are known as phobias like fear of darkness, fear of enclosed spaces, fear of open spaces, fear of heights, fear of animals, fear of devils and ghosts, fear of thieves, fear of enemies, fear of charms, illusory fears of being attacked or killed by someone lurking in the background.

The worries and suffering which a person experiences are nothing more than the interaction of his selfish desire with changing worldly conditions. The failure to understand this fact is the cause of much suffering. But for a person who has trained his mind to realise the real nature of life and its characteristics, he has indeed made progress in overcoming his suffering. He realises that departure or separation from pleasant experiences and those whom he loves are unavoidable. This can happen at any time, whether at the start of a career, at the middle or even at the end. The only certainty in this uncertain world is things must come to an end. So a person who thinks he is indispensable or that he must be around to see what is to be done, should consider what will happen when he is no longer around. He will be missed and his absence will be felt perhaps for a short period of time. Since no one is indispensable in this world, the world will still go on as usual without him. If that be so, then why should he worry himself so much, harbouring imaginary fears that only harm his health and eventually shorten the period towards the end of life's journey – Death!

The separation of togetherness also brings suffering. A person feels lost, dejected, hopeless and frustrated when someone beloved leaves him or her. This is a natural process. People experience suffering whenever they are rejected by those whom they love. But sometimes instead of learning to cope with the situation by allowing time to heal the wounds, they become paralysed with dejection, pondering about it over and over in their minds, looking for ways and means to mend their broken hearts. Some even express their anger and frustration through violent methods.

Fear and Superstition

There is yet another kind of fear that stalks the human mind. It is the fear of the uncontrollable forces of nature and of the unknown. This fear has dogged man through the ages as he learned to deal with wild beasts and protect himself from the attacks of other tribes. In that long night of savagery, in that constant effort to deal with the forces of nature, the seeds of superstition were sown in the human mind. And this superstition has persisted and been passed down from generation to generation up to the present day.

Fear in its primitive sense is described as an intense emotional reaction characterised by attempts to flee from the situation which elicits it and by physiological changes such as blanching, tremors, rapid heart beat, dryness of mouth, etc. According to a well known psychologist John Broadus Watson, *fear is one of the three unlearned emotional reactions, the others being love and anger.* Watson's view is that fear is induced in the newborn by a sudden loss of support or by loud noises. Even the infant, he believes, must receive affection and re-assurance, ' mothering ' may ease the tensions arising from basal anxiety. It is believed that certain fears in a new born infant could be those associated with its previous existence which have been brought forward and still remain fresh and vivid in its mind and that visions relating to such previous fears do sometimes manifest themselves from time to time during early infancy.

When faced with forces beyond his comprehension, the difference between the savage and the beast becomes apparent. The beast adapts itself instinctively and succumbs to this force. The savage, on the other hand, when surrounded by wild beasts stronger than himself, or when confronted by the forces of nature like rain, wind, thunder and lightning or natural calamities like earthquakes, volcanic eruptions or epidemic diseases, will prostrate himself in all terror on the ground, pleading protection from unknown powers. From his early perception of a power outside himself, which he thought could be appeased through prayer, just as he himself could be pleased, the savage developed ritual and worship and made the forces of nature as his gods. Good forces became good ' gods ' while evil forces became evil 'gods'.

Fear comes to those who are unable to comprehend the basic laws of nature. Either as a principle or motive, fear is the beginning of superstitious beliefs. The notion of incurring the displeasure of a Creator is instilled into the minds of the followers of many religions who depend on the concept of God for the fulfilment of everything. The foundation of some religious systems and worship is based on the instinctive fear of the unknown. The fear created by religions is the worst form of fear since it imprisons and ensnares the mind. Fear fertilizes the growth of superstition that flourishes in the fog of ignorance.

Man yearns for security for himself and for those whom he loves in this world of constant flux which could offer no permanent solution to his problems. The moment he thinks he has solved a particular problem, the conditions surrounding the original circumstances will change and yet another set of problems will then emerge, leaving him confused and lost as ever before. He is anxious, like a child who builds sand-castles on the beach and is afraid of every wave that comes in.

In this craving for security and fear of death, man falls prey to superstition. Surrounded by the mystery of the universe, he develops faith in things that he fears. It is ignorance and fear of the unknown that gave rise to early religious beliefs, and the workings of the universe are explained in terms of infallible supernatural gods who are supposed to control everything that happens. Even though science has done much to dispel such myths and improve the knowledge of modern man, much of the superstitions inherited from the past still continue to remain with him and he has yet to break himself free from this self imposed bondage. Superstitions weaken and enslave the mind. Superstitious ideas, beliefs and practices are ingrained not only amongst uneducated people but strangely also the well-educated as well.

Society should recall the words of the Buddha who said: *'Wheresoever fear arises, it arises in the fool, and not in the wise man.'*

What does Worry Do to Us?

'When envy, hate, and fear are habitual,' says Dr. Alexis Carrel, 'they are capable of starting genuine diseases'. Medical science is of the view that diseases like diabetes, high blood pressure, gastric ulcers, skin diseases and asthma are aggravated, if not actually brought about from anxiety and worry. Thought can generate organic disorders as we tend to attract what we expect in life. Doctors find that their patients tend to heal in accordance with their own expectations, rather than healing as the prognosis would suggest. Mental suffering profoundly disrupts good health. Businessmen who do not know how to cope with worry and stressful situations often die young. Those who remain calm and maintain their inner peace in spite of the external turmoil of worldly life are insulated from nervous and organic disorders.

Experience has shown that a good deal of physical and mental ill-health can be traced to worry. Worry dries up blood sooner than age. Some degree of fear, worry and anxiety is natural and may even be necessary for self-preservation, but when it is not under control, constant fear and prolonged worry will only wreak havoc on the human organism. These factors all contribute to the weakening of our normal bodily functions.

According to medical opinion, in the treatment of most functional disorders, close attention has to be paid to the mental condition of the patient. They have also realised that worries do not solve problems but instead only aggravate them which in turn will cause one's physical and mental ruin. In addition, a person who is perpetually worried creates an unhealthy atmosphere at home, in the office and in society in general. Through rash actions arising from his personal worry and anxiety, he upsets the peace and happiness of others around him.

Just as worry is capable of causing so much harm to oneself and others, so also is fear. Persistent fear keeps a person in a state of perpetual mental tension and anguish. Fear progressively erodes life and debases the mind. Fear is a potent pessimistic force which darkens the future. If a man harbours any kind of fear, his way of thinking will be affected. This unwholesome mental state is capable of eroding his personality and making him landlord to a ghost.

So great a hold has fear upon us that it has rightly been described as humanity's arch-enemy. Fear has become a fixed mental state amongst millions of people. To live in continued dread, cringing, and haunted by the fear of devils, spooks, gods and goddesses is the common lot of humanity wallowing in ignorance.

Fear can however turn to panic in cases of unexpected crises when there are no preparations for meeting the threat.

2

OUR TROUBLES

A difficult situation can be handled in two ways: We can either do something to change it, or face it. If we can do something, then why worry and get upset over it – just change it. If there is nothing we can do, again, why worry and get upset over it? Things will not get better with anger and worry. ~ *Shantideva* ~

Life is a continuous journey beset with problems. As long as we live in this world, problems and troubles will always be a part and parcel of human experience. On some occasions, we may be blessed with gain, fame, praise or happiness; and we may also face the unfavourable situations of loss, ill-fame, blame and pain. Life swings like a pendulum. One moment, it swings towards favourable conditions which we receive so heartily; at another moment, it swings towards unfavourable conditions which we so desperately seek to avoid.

Instead of understanding worldly conditions, as what they really are, people sometimes have the tendency to magnify their troubles. This is similar to the saying 'making a mountain out of a molehill.' When people lose someone or something they love, they feel that they will never be able to be happy again. When disturbed and harassed by people who are insensitive to their needs, they feel that they have never before been so harshly treated. And they carry that hurt in their minds, clinging to the pain needlessly and continuing to suffer with those thoughts. Would it not be better to let go of such thoughts and realise that since all conditioned things must one day come to an end, so the unfavourable situations they are experiencing will also pass away?

We should understand that there is a way out of the suffering and problems we face in this life. None is hopelessly condemned to eternal misery, unless he himself allows it to be so. It is important to realise that all conditioned phenomena, including suffering and all problems, arise out of causes and that nothing can arise by way of independent causes. Having realised this, we can put an end to each and every form of suffering by discovering the root causes of our problems.

Facing Problems

We should not be disheartened when faced with problems, but instead act wisely in overcoming them. No worldly-minded person can ever be free from problems. Hence, it is not so much who experiences problems that marks the difference between a wise and an unwise person, but the manner in which he faces them.

Socrates, whose wife was reputed to be hot-tempered would always find fault with him and used to nag him almost daily. One day, when she had finished all what she had to say, Socrates complimented her saying that compared to previous occasions, she had on that particular day shown some improvement in her diction and style of speech.

This shows how a wise person should face false accusation and blame in a humourous way.

Pandit Nehru once said: *'We have to face problems and try to solve them. We have to face them, certainly, on a spiritual background; but not run away from them in the name of spiritualism.'*

Ella Wilcox gives her viewpoint on smiling one's way out of troubles.

'It's easy enough to be pleasant;
When life flows like a song,
But the man worthwhile,
Is the one who can smile,
When things go dead wrong.
For the test of the heart is trouble

And it always comes with the years,
And the smile that is worth
The praises of earth,
Is the smile that shines through the tears.'

Dr. Rabindranath Tagore, a well-known Indian poet, explains in a prayer, the approach to face problems without harbouring fear or worry.

'Let me not pray to be sheltered from dangers,
But be fearless in facing them.
Let me not beg for the stilling of my pain,
But for the heart to conquer it.
Let me not crave in anxious fear to be saved,
But hope for the patience to win my freedom.'

Something unpleasant happens, say, our favourite thing or possession is lost or is accidentally broken. There are two ways of reacting to the loss and damage. We can either choose to brood over it, by blaming either ourselves or others. Or we can pass it off by saying 'The thing is gone. It is bad enough to have lost it, but why should we allow it to make us unhappy to suffer the loss and damage?' It would be useful to trace back to the causes that had led to the breakage and loss so as to avoid such an occurrence in the future. We can also think about how the loss can be replaced, or how to avert whatever problems that may arise from that loss. If the loss is of no real conse-quence to others, we may even start to do something else to take our mind from the incident, since it is in the nature of compounded things that such occurrences happen. Should an unfortunate thing happen and if it is beyond our control, then with the support of our understanding of the nature of life, we must have the courage to face it.

In other words, adopt a positive frame of mind when faced with such problems, rather than let it dwell on negative states. If unhappiness should arise due to a negative frame of mind it is really of our own doing or seeking.

According to the Buddha, '*Mind is the forerunner of all states. Mind is chief; mind-made are these states.*' The Buddha also taught that our sorrows are caused by our own actions and arise from our own ignorance. He showed us how to remove sorrow, but we ourselves must work to gain happiness.

Developing Courage and Understanding

All negative forces can be uprooted by the correct method of meditation or mental culture as taught by the Buddha, because the untrained mind is the main cause of such illness or problems. The Buddha had said that the mind is very hard to perceive, extremely subtle and it wanders at will. A wise person will guard it as a guarded mind is conducive to happiness.

It is common for people to blame others for their worries, especially when they do not find a solution to their problems. Under these circumstances, it is so convenient to find a scapegoat: someone who could be blamed for those problems and on whom grievances could be vented. When a child is hurt it starts to cry. To stop it from crying and to make it feel better, its mother pretends to hit another person just to show the child that he or she had been responsible for having caused it to cry. The child being satisfied that its vengeance had been accomplished stops crying and starts to smile. This clearly shows that the taking of revenge on someone gives satisfaction to the ordinary human mind.

It is always hard to admit one's shortcomings, and so easy to lay the blame on someone else. In fact, some would even take pleasure in doing so but it is a wrong attitude to adopt. When faced with a similar situation, we should not be resentful or angry with others. We should do our utmost in a painstaking and calm way to solve our own problems. It is always good to remember that while others can create disturbances which provide conditions for the arising of worries within us, no one can create worries in our mind if we know how to guard ourselves well.

In the Dhammapada, the Buddha said: '*Your worst enemy cannot harm you as much as your own mind, unguarded. But once mastered, no one can help you as much, not even your father, mother or any other relative.*'

The following injunctions by a well-known poet can help us to face our troubles with courage and without harbouring resentment in our hearts.

Have faith in you

'If you keep your head, while all about you
Are losing theirs and blaming it on you;
If you can trust yourself when others doubt you,
But make allowances for their doubting too;

'If you can wait and not be tired by waiting,
Or being lied about and not deal in lies,
Or being hated and not give way to hating,
Nor yet look too good, nor talk too wise;

'If you can dream and not make dreams your Master,
If you can think and not make thought your aim;
If you can meet with Triumph and Disaster
And treat those two imposters just the same;

'If you can make one heap of all your winnings
And risk it in one turn of pitch-and-toss,
And lose and start again at the beginning,
And not breathe a word about your loss;

'If you can bear to hear the truth you've spoken
Twisted by knaves to make a trap for fools,
Or see the things you give your life to, broken
And stop to build them up again with worn-out tools;

'If you can force your heart and nerve and sinews
To serve their turn long after they are done,
And so hold on when there is nothing in you
Except the will which says to them, "Hold on!"

'If you can talk with crowds and keep your virtue,
Or walk with Kings and not lose the common touch;
If neither foes or loving friends can hurt you
And all men count with you, but none too much;

'If you can fill the unforgiving minute
With sixty seconds worth of distance run,
Yours is the Earth and everything that's in it
And, what is more, you'll be a man, My Son!'

When we are faced with fear, considerable courage is required to recognise the truth of its origin, and still greater courage to accept that truth after we have experienced it. We attract what we fear and when we confront fears they disappear. Getting that fear out into the open and frankly facing it is of primary importance. If we can objectively trace the origin of the fear, we would have won half the battle of overcoming it.

When faced with worries, we should not wear a sulky face and exhibit it to the rest of the world. Everyone has enough of his or her own problems, without having to add on something extra from someone else. If we like we could confide our problems with another person or speak to someone who can really help us, but not add to the misery of one who cannot.

Do we have the courage and strength to maintain a smile when facing difficulties? It is not really difficult, if we were to reduce the egoism which leads one to believe that only he or she alone needs comforting. In addition, we should also count our blessings rather than shortcomings. Always remember the saying, '*I complained that I had no shoes until I met a man who had no feet.*' When we think thus, we will realise that there are many people who may be in an even worse position than we ourselves, and against this understanding our own problem can be reduced accordingly.

Thinking of others rather than brooding over our own problems is also a way of being happy. The person who is busy making others happy will have no time to think of his own selfish needs.

A noted British anatomist was once asked by a student: 'What is the best cure for fear?' His answer was, '*Try doing something for someone.*' The student was considerably astonished and requested for further clarification. In reply the instructor said, 'You can't have two opposing sets of thoughts in your mind at one and the same time. One set of thoughts will always drive the other out. If, for instance, your mind is completely occupied with an unselfish desire to help someone else, you can't be harbouring fear at the same time.' This notion that it is impossible to have a wholesome thought and an unwholesome thought at one and the same time has been pointed out in the Buddha's teachings. By constantly striving to develop a wholesome state of mind, we can leave no room for delusion or fear to take root. In addition, we will also be able to maintain a warm feeling of having done something useful for another.

An important step in controlling the mind is the

disciplining of the body and speech. The five sense organs namely eyes, nose, tongue, ears, and body — provide living beings with sense-information from their environment. The eyes see objects which create thoughts. Likewise, the ears are drawn to sounds and the nose to smells which also create thoughts. Arising from the sense information of seeing, hearing, smelling, tasting and touching, the mind distinguishes that which is pleasant, unpleasant and neutral. In addition, it also dictates what the body should do in response to the same signal. Most people respond to their sense-objects spontaneously, developing attachment to pleasant objects and aversion to unpleasant objects. There are very few people who are not controlled by these conditioned responses.

One must learn to control one's thoughts in order to have a better control over one's body and speech. Thoughts can be classified as wholesome and unwholesome. Wholesome thoughts are those that contribute to the development of a positive character, proper attitude and right behaviour. Such thoughts are conducive to the benefit and well-being of mankind. On the other hand, thoughts which undermine the development of a positive individual and contribute to the detriment of mankind are unwholesome thoughts.

One should learn to recognize the nature of one's thoughts as they arise from moment to moment, distinguishing the wholesome thoughts from the unwholesome ones. Once a person has developed the facility of watching his thoughts, he has made a significant headway in nurturing wholesome thoughts. If the thoughts in his mind are unwholesome, he applies right effort to remove such unwholesome thoughts, and at the same time prevents the arising of such thoughts. If the thoughts are wholesome, he uses right effort to cultivate and promote such thoughts. In other words, through the cultivation of awareness of one's thoughts, a person can learn to have control over the mind instead of being reactive to sense impulses fed by his senses.

The process of disciplining the body and purifying speech and mind brings happiness. Everyone wants to live happily, and happiness is everyone's birthright. To achieve happiness to which one is entitled, we should practise the self-cleansing process prescribed by the Buddha:

1) To discard all unwholesome thoughts that have arisen;
2) To eliminate unwholesome thoughts as they arise;
3) To nurture wholesome thoughts that have arisen by putting them into daily practice; and
4) To cultivate wholesome thoughts that have not yet arisen.

These four simple guidelines can easily be practised in our daily lives. This is one of the ways to maintain a healthy mind which everyone can follow. Although many may choose not to follow it but would prefer to give in to the dictates of their craving, desire and aversion, we should not follow suit if we sincerely wish to have happiness. It is never too late to start practising self-awareness and discipline to cultivate a positive, wholesome and creative mind. Anytime is a good time to start, especially starting from now.

Putting Problems in Their Proper Perspective

Sometimes when we are faced with a serious problem, we feel depressed with its seeming magnitude and weight. When this happens, it is profitable to wander out in the evening and look up at the sky. We see countless numbers of stars. From outer space, the sun in our solar system will only appear as one of the innumerable number of stars. If the sun were to disappear suddenly from space, would its absence be noticed from outer space?

Our world is only a tiny speck in the universe. What if we were to disappear from the world, would it be of any universal significance? Our loved ones and friends of course will miss us for a time, but besides them, maybe no one else would. But compared to ourselves, how much smaller are our troubles? When we consider the vastness of the universe with the tiny speck which the Sun is and the tinier speck which we call the world, and our troubles will appear very minute indeed in comparison.

If we can see our problems in this perspective, we would understand the first step of the Noble Eightfold Path, that is, Right Viewpoint. This can also mean a right sense of values, that is, by not thinking that we are more important than we really are. And if we can develop this viewpoint, we will know what things in life matter and what do not, and that our troubles which come and go are of no real significance. Ponder for a moment the significance of the undermentioned valuable saying in Islam.

> *'Faith is the source of my power.*
> *Sorrow is my friend.*
> *Knowledge is my weapon.*
> *Patience is my Garb and Virtue'*

> ~ *Prophet Mohammad* ~

Troubles will soon pass. What had caused you to burst into tears today will soon be forgotten tomorrow. You may perhaps remember that you cried, but maybe not the exact circumstances which caused the tears. As we go through life, we waste so much mental energy when we lie awake at night, brooding over something that had upset us during the day. We nurse resentment against someone and keep running the same thoughts over and over again through our mind. But is it not so that while we may fall into a rage about something now, that after some time has elapsed and other problems arise which would seem to be more pressing, we may begin to wonder what it was that in the first place we were so angry about? If we reflect on past resentments, we will be surprised to find how we have deliberately continued to be unhappy when we could have in fact put that unhappiness to a stop by doing or thinking about something else.

Whatever our troubles, however pressing they may appear, time will heal our wounds. But besides leaving things to time, surely there must be something we can do to prevent ourselves from being hurt in the first place. We could maintain our peace of mind by not allowing people or troubles to drain our energies away since it is ourselves and not others who create our unhappiness.

We gain academic knowledge without personal experience. Armed with academic knowledge some young people think they can solve all the world's problems. Science can provide the material things to solve our problems, but it cannot help us to solve our spiritual problems. There is no substitute for wise people who have experienced the world. Think about this saying, "When I was 18, I thought what a fool my father was. Now that I am 28, I am surprised how much the old man has learned in 10 years!" It is not the father that has learned, rather it is you who have learned to see things in a mature way.

3

WHY DO WE SUFFER?

The cause of suffering is nothing but selfish desire, friction between elements and energies and changes.

~ Buddha ~

There was none so intimately aware of and concerned with human suffering than the Buddha. It may be useful to look into his life and his search into the cause and cure for universal suffering.

As a prince, Siddhartha led a sheltered life amidst the splendour, beauty and security of his palace. He knew no discomfort, only ease and luxury. Day and night, he was entertained by beautiful maids and attendants, by court musicians and enticing dancers. He had everything a man would want of earthly pleasures, yet he felt a void in his princely life.

While venturing out of the palace one day, Siddhartha saw four sights, which may be ordinary to our eyes but which to him had a great impact. He saw on separate occasions an old man, a sick man, a dead man and a mendicant or monk. These four sights made a deep impression on him, as he had seen them for the first time in his adult life. He was shocked at the nature of worldly suffering humans are subjected to after having witnessed the first three sights. It reminded him that old age, sickness, and finally, death, were the common lot of humanity, and that he too would one day have to face the same fate.

However, it was the sight of a mendicant, which gave him the hope of deliverance. It gave him the inspiration and courage to renounce his regal position and all worldly pleasures to seek the Truth that would help suffering humanity.

One night he turned his back on material possessions and went in search of the universal answers to the problems of existence. That was the night when he left the palace quietly, dressed only in a single robe. For six long years, he hardly knew where to go or to rest. He had no companions and no proper meals, except what the people gave him. He ate from the alms bowl like a common beggar. Having been used to a life of luxury, he almost threw up at the first sight of the jumble of coarse food in his bowl which the poor people had offered him. But he endured it all – the food, the blazing sun, the drenching rain, and the cold nights in the forest – and wandered barefooted from place to place, from teacher to teacher in search of the truth.

The Truth finally dawned upon him six years later while seated under the Bodhi tree. During his search, he came to share the whole vast spectrum of human experiences. He learned about unsatisfactoriness not only from his life of abundant luxury, but also by following for a while the way of the ascetics who tortured their bodies under the belief that wisdom and freedom could be attained through such practices. He almost died from such practices which ultimately proved futile. He also tried to learn from the best teachers who willingly taught him, but who were unable to give the answers he sought.

Realising that he had to find the Truth through his own effort, he gave up self-torture and followed the Middle Path of avoiding the extremes of indulgent luxury and self-torture. With perseverance and un-failing determination, he gained Buddhahood through his own persevering effort.

The Buddha discovered that Suffering, which is caused by desire, could be put to an end by following the Noble Eightfold Path. Through this Path, suffer-ing could be ended completely. Having understood completely the nature of life, the Buddha dedicated the rest of his life to teach what he had discovered to all who would listen to him and understand.

The Nature of Life

The Buddha saw suffering as suffering, and happiness as happiness. This is not what unenlightened minds would see. Generally, most people dislike having to face the true facts of life. They lull themselves into a false sense of security by day-dreaming and imagination, taking the shadow for the substance. Many never see, know or even care to find out the facts of life, preferring to live a humdrum existence in the world to which they are born.

If we examine the actual state of humanity, it is clear that this state is marked by unsatisfactoriness throughout. Every living being, human or otherwise, throughout the whole universe is struggling for existence through a never ending battle for survival. The brief moments of happiness come to an end with the onset of sickness, old age and death.

Goethe, the great German poet, dramatist and philosopher, once said that *if he were to count all the days of real happiness he had during his life time they would only add up to no more than a fortnight in duration.*

However ingeniously we might plan and organise our society and adjust human relationships, so long as the world remains what it is even the best of us cannot escape suffering. Even if, by some stroke of good fortune, we manage to evade the usual irritants of life, we cannot free ourselves from death. Our bodily organism has in it the seeds of dissolution. Mortality is native to our world of component things. The thought of death as the end to all existence would be unendurable to the ignorant who is caught in the web of worldly existence and engrossed in the enjoyment of the fleeting life which he mistakenly thinks is permanent.

The danger of refusing to face facts and accept the truths of life, such as old age and death, is that it makes a person suffer even more, not less, in the long run. Recollection on the inevitability of death, accompanied with the right attitude of mind, gives a person courage to lead a purposeful life and calmness during periods of sorrow and at the time of death.

Unsatisfactoriness follows man like his shadow along the pathway of life. During childhood, he has to shoulder the demands of duty. In the prime of manhood, he struggles ceaselessly to support himself and his family in answer to his responsibilities. The declining years bring sickness, weakness, dependency, loneliness, suffering, and finally, death. Such is the fate of all humanity.

It is sheer folly to expect security or eternal happiness while one sojourns in a world subject to constant change. People work hard and undergo much suffering in order to have a little bit of pleasure. But they would have to give up fleeting pleasures if they wish to secure permanent happiness. If man wishes to put an end to suffering, he must eradicate his own selfishness and cultivate contentment.

Understanding the Facts of Life

Those who have not studied the Buddha's teachings cannot understand what is meant by the statement that existence creates suffering. Reflect on this: Every creature which lives on earth either preys on other animals or is itself being preyed upon. All creatures either hunt or are hunted by others. Even herbivorous animals live in fear because they are the victims of other animals and human beings. No one can escape from this eternal battle for survival which creates suffering, fear of death and uncertainty in life. The turning point in the Buddha's life came when he was still a prince. One day he observed that a frog was swallowed by a snake. Just then a hawk swooped down and carried both the snake and frog away. The prince reflected upon this phenomenon and observed that all existence is sorrowful because living beings try to escape from each other. At the same time, they prey on others for survival. It is difficult to understand why all these innocent beings should suffer if they were created by an all powerful, compassionate creator. How could such a creator allow his creatures to be preyed upon by others and to live in constant fear?

In the world marked with unsatisfactoriness, the Buddha makes no pretence of offering stability in conditions and things which are essentially unstable. Some people who do not understand this call him a pessimist. They are not unlike a child who builds a sand castle near the sea and regards any prediction of its dissolution with the rising tide as pessimism. But the Buddha offers something infinitely better than the stability which people foolishly seek in unstable worldly phenomena. He offers them a method of attaining ultimate stability, Nibbana, which is eternally peaceful and secure.

Worldly conditions, according to Buddhism, are impermanent and unsatisfactory. The current wave of discontentment which man is caught up with is mainly due to a lack of understanding of the fleeting nature of worldly life. Many of us do not know this nature at all. Even if we do, we habitually fail to apply it to our daily lives. In our ignorance, we blame the government, society or everybody else except ourselves. As cultured people, we ought to know that our egoism and ignorance are to be blamed. What hinders us from realising the TRUTH is our selfishness, our pride, hatred and ignorance. These defilements appear to be so real that our power to believe in the Truth is crippled.

We do not like the truth because sometimes it is unpleasant, inconvenient, or it does not support our craving. There is no other more important injunction in the world, nor one with a deeper hidden meaning, than the phrase (used by Shakespeare in Hamlet) *'To thine own self be true.'* In other words, be true to your own conscience. Whether we accept the Truth that craving causes sorrow or not does not and cannot alter the basic principles of the universe. We can recognise the difference between right and wrong, but through our ignorance and foolishness, we rationalise or give a thousand reasons for failing to perceive that difference. With our intelligence, we can justify our actions for any wrongful actions committed, but in the final analysis, it is better to call a spade a spade. We must be like a good surgeon who can locate the source of a cancerous growth and remove it. The operation is painful, but once the diseased part is removed, our chances of enjoying good health are vastly enhanced.

Fleeting Happiness

Life is unsatisfactory because it is impermanent. Henri Bergson, the French philosopher, says, *'To exist is to change; to change is to mature; to mature is to go on creating oneself endlessly.'* So, those suffering and despairing ones who seek light and guidance should not base their hopes of happiness on a life whose elements are in a flux as the shifting sands of a river mouth.

When a person has a happy life, he would like the passage of time to stand still. This ceaseless passage of time is so obvious a quality of our lives that we take it for granted. Within this ceaseless movement, all things we know are born, grow, decay and die, and we will go through this process with them.

'Life is uncertain,' says the Buddha, *'but death is certain.'*

The law of impermanence lays its cruel hands on all people. And all youth ends in old age, all health in sickness, all strength in impotence, all beauty in ugliness, and all life in death. Nothing can stop this process. Death follows birth, as night follows day. This process of change is common to all – to the poor and the rich alike, to the young and the old. But this seems to be the very thing some of us forget, living and acting as if we are immortal.

If we look closely at life, we can see how it is continually changing and moving between contacts. We will notice how it fluctuates between rise and fall, success and failure, gain and loss, honour and contempt, praise and blame. We see more clearly how our hearts would respond to happiness and sorrow, delight and despair, satisfaction and disappointment, hope and fear.

These mighty waves of emotion carry us up, but no sooner are we up in the crest when, they fling us down. Hardly have we found some rest, before we are swept up again by the power of a new wave. How can we expect to gain a footing on the crest of the waves? Where shall we erect the building of life in the midst of this ever restless ocean of existence, if not on the island of equanimity which will shelter us from every storm? This island of equanimity develops in our minds after we have undergone many disappointments, and have finally emerged much wiser. It is an island which provides stability and peace in the face of sickness, separation and death.

The Picture of Life

Even our pleasure is the basis of unsatisfactoriness. If we are seeking the Truth, we must recognise this fact, whether we like it or not. This may be unpleasant at first sight, but if we give it up because of that unpleasantness, we will not get very far in the search for Truth. We will be blinded by *Maya* – illusion.

It may not be easy to accept this version of the world which seems at times so fair. And yet, when we look around, we see that even in the beauty of spring, many die and many more suffer from incurable diseases. We experience disappointments, frustrations, miseries and suffering in various forms.

Gradually, as we grow in years and experience, this vision of a world in constant flux widens, if we are not wilfully blind. Looking still deeper beneath the surface of life, we can profit and learn from the events in the lives of people we know. We see how even a happy ending may prove to be but a sad beginning, or how a slight indiscretion or weakness may ruin a man's whole life.

Therefore uncertainty in everything is certain. This understanding can console our unsatisfied minds.

Worlds on worlds are rolling ever
From creation to decay
Like the bubbles on a river
Sparkling, bursting borne away.

~ Shelley ~

A Tibetan Buddhist yogi and poet, Milarepa, gives this simple but comprehensive picture of human life.

'Youth is like a summer flower –
Suddenly it fades away.
Old age is like a fire spreading
Through the fields – suddenly, it's at your heels.
The Buddha once said, 'Birth and death
Are like sunrise and sunset
Now come, now go.'

Sickness is like a little bird
Wounded by a sling.
Know you not, health and strength
Will in time desert you?
Death is like a dry oil lamp
(After its last flicker)
This world is impermanent;
Nothing, I assure you
Can remain unchanging.
Evil karma is like a waterfall
Which I have never seen flow upward,

A sinful man is like a poisonous tree –
If you lean on it, you will injured be.
Transgressors are like frost-bitten peas –
Like spoilt fat, they ruin everything.
Dharma practisers are like peasants cultivating in
the fields.

The Law of Karma is like Samsara's wheel –
Whoever breaks it will suffer a great loss.

Samsara is like a poisonous thorn
In the flesh – if not pulled out,
The poison will increase and spread.

The coming of death is like the shadow
Of a tree at sunset –
It runs fast and none can halt it.
When that time comes,
What else can help but the Holy Dharma?

Though Dharma is the fount of Victory,
Those who aspire to it are rare.
Scores of men are tangled in
The miseries of Samsara
Into this misfortune born,
They strive by plunder and theft for gain.
When you are strong and healthy
You ne'er think of sickness coming,
But it descends with sudden force
Like a stroke of lightning.

When involved in worldly things
You ne'er think of death's approach
Quick it comes like thunder
Crashing round your head.

Sickness, old age and death
Ever meet each other
As do hands and mouth
Do you not fear the miseries
You experienced in the past?
Surely you will feel much pain
If misfortunes attack you?

The woes of life succeed one another
Like the sea's incessant waves –
One has barely passed, before
The next one takes its place.
Until you are liberated, pain
And pleasure come and go at random
Like passers-by encountered in the street.

Pleasures are precarious,
Like bathing in the sun;
Transient, too, as the snow storms
Which come without warning.
Remembering these things,
Why not practise the Dharma?'

~ *Songs of Milarepa* ~

Can We Satisfy Desire?

It is hardly surprising that today, in our so-called highly advanced society, dominated by greed, hatred, suspicion and fear, an increasing number of people should feel loneliness, frustration, jealousy and enmity, and are unable to see any meaning in life. Youths today demonstrate this inability to see meaning in life in various ways, which range from delinquency to drug addiction.

The enemy of mankind is selfish craving. Through this all evils come to living beings. People are always craving for pleasures, wealth and property. They are deluded with the idea that happiness consists of the satisfaction of their desires. Such a belief is particularly prevalent in a materialistic society such as ours. While the fulfilment of our needs and desires, which cause no harm to others, does bring some form of happiness, one should not be led into thinking that sensual gratification is the only source of happiness nor does it constitute the highest form of happiness. A person who subscribes to such thinking will lead a life of non-fulfilment, like chasing after rainbows.

Certain things give us pleasure, so we try to hold on to them and increase their quantity. Some other things bring displeasure, so we try to avoid or remove them. Unless we can have mastery and control over the forces of desire and aversion, they will drive us from one unhappy experience to another. Desire and aversion operate together: at one moment it is aversion in action, at another moment it is desire.

When hunger or thirst arises, there springs a feeling of discomfort. Subsequently, desire springs up to allay that discomfort. All our desires are like that. They start from some discomfort or a feeling that something is lacking. And then we search for things that we think can fill that aching void. If we do not get what we want, the feeling of void continues to ache. If, however, we succeed in getting it, the desire or hunger becomes satisfied, and for a time, ceases to exist. Even so, the pleasure of anticipation disappears, and we feel somehow cheated and disappointed because what we experience is never quite what we expected. And so, new desires and anticipations are created. This continual arising and search for the satisfaction of desires is the basis that constitutes mundane, human life.

Some people spend their whole life accumulating material things: no amount of accumulation can make them contented. The desire for more and more is their whole life's devotion. When they fail to get what they seek, they become disappointed. But even after getting the things they have so desperately worked for, they may turn out to be just as disappointed as before. The object of their dreams appears to be less wonderful, less appealing or desirable than they had earlier considered it to be. By now, their desires and expectations have gone up by a few notches, and they are not satisfied with their new acquisitions. They are constantly egged on by the notion that the 'grass is always greener on the other side of the fence'. People such as these can never be happy or contented. In fact, the more they have, the greater their desire becomes. It is said that man's needs, such as food, shelter and clothing, can be satisfied, but seldom his desires.

Pleasure is not Happiness

Many people have the mistaken idea that they can solve all their problems with money. While money is necessary for one to lead a comfortable life in modern society, it does not always solve one's problems. Not only that, it also creates new problems as well. Therefore, it is important for us to put things as well as our lives in proper perspective. When we realise the true value and nature of things and reduce our craving for sensual gratification, we will have more peace arising from simplicity and contentment.

To satisfy their craving and hatred, people create problems for themselves and others. Nations go to war for this reason. They hope to defeat others and conquer their lands. Battles and wars were fought and stories of enormous suffering have been recorded in the annals of world history. But human beings, entangled in worldliness, will not come to their senses so easily. They suffer so much misery and face many dangers, but yet will not wake up to reality. They are like the camel which loves to eat thorny bushes. The more thorns it eats, the more the blood which gushes from its mouth. Still it continues eating thorny plants and will not give them up. In fact the worldly pleasure that people experience is like eating a hot potato.

The Buddha taught that all our miseries arise from wanting the wrong sort of things: more money for self indulgence, power over other people, and cherishing the idea of living on forever after one is dead. The desire for these things makes people become discontented with life. This is especially the case when they think only about their own interest, and disregard others' welfare. When they do not get what they want, they become restless and discontented. At the same time when we gain what we were longing and praying for we experience unsatisfactoriness or disappointment because of the fear of losing it.

All our mental sufferings are caused by selfish

desires for pleasure. Think about that. They are caused by the desire to be what we are not, to have what we do not have, and not to have the things we already have. If we think hard and long about it, there is no denying that the chief culprit in our inability to enjoy a sense of happiness is desire.

What is fear but the desire to avoid; greed, the desire to have; jealousy, the desire that others shall not have; grief, the desire to regain something or someone. All our negative emotions can be worked out in terms of desire, the chain that binds us. The only way to avoid this restlessness is to reduce or get rid of the desire that causes it. This may be difficult to do, but not impossible. When a man overcomes restlessness, he arrives at a state of calmness or contentment.

The Buddha has said: *'The joy of pleasure in the world, and those of heaven are not worth a sixteenth part of the joy arising from the destruction of craving.'*

Here is another saying from a writer for you to ponder:

'Sorry is he whose burden is heavy,
And happy is he who has cast it down;
When once he has cast off his burden,
He will seek to be burdened no more.'

Suffering, which is the price we pay for our existence, is brought about by craving. As a result of craving, we perform actions which leave imprints or seeds stored in our minds. Later in this life or another, the seeds of our actions will ripen as reactions. In other words, selfish craving creates kamma which gives rise to reactions. Our past actions, coupled by other factors, cause the good and bad we experience today.

Contemplate on Yourself

As people go through life, some learn to age gracefully and accumulate wisdom born from experience. They realise that to crave is to be subjected to more suffering, and the cure for suffering lies not in appealing to the gods for help but by finding salvation within themselves.

However, the person with a worldly nature suffers so much sorrow and affliction. In his youth, he tries to fill his days with enjoyment. But before he knows it, the years have passed and he has grown old. He is distressed to find that while his body has become unfit as an instrument for pleasure, his heart is still youthful in its craving. These are the people whose craving grows with their age: the older they grow, the stronger their craving becomes. This being the case, their suffering will correspondingly be greater.

One reason for failing to control craving is the pride in man. Under the false sense of pride, people go about committing evil deeds and refuse to recognise the obvious. By the same token, we should avoid maintaining pride in youth while still young, pride in health while still healthy, and pride in life while still living a good life.

Some people, without considering their real positions, think that they are higher than all others. They are so full of themselves that they develop a grandiose opinion of themselves. This can be dangerous because 'Pride always goes before a fall'.

******

The proud beetle in a lump of cowdung. There once was a beetle which came upon a lump of cowdung. He worked himself into it and liking what he saw, he invited his friends to join him in building a city in it. After working feverishly for a few days they built a magnificent 'city' in the dung and feeling very proud of their achievement they decided to elect the first beetle as their king. Now to honour their new 'king' they organised a grand parade through their 'city'. While these impressive proceedings were taking place, an elephant happened to pass by and seeing the lump of cow dung he lifted his foot to avoid stepping on it. The king beetle saw the elephant and angrily shouted at the huge beast. 'Hey you! Don't you have any respect for royalty? Don't you know it is rude to lift your leg over my majestic head? Apologise at once or I'll have you punished.' The elephant looked down and said, 'Your most gracious majesty, I humbly crave your pardon.' Thus saying he knelt down on the lump of cow dung and crushed king, city, citizens and pride in one act of obeisance.

******

The Buddha, overcame these three kinds of pride when he saw the four sights. When he saw the old man, the pride in youth left him. When he saw the sick man, the pride in health left him. When he saw the dead man, the pride in life left him. If we remove these three types of pride from our minds, we will not be shocked and distressed when we encounter these states. It is useful to contemplate:

- *I am liable to old age; I have not outstripped old age.*
- *I am liable to disease; I have not outstripped disease.*
- *I am liable to death; I have not outstripped death.*
- *Among all that is near and dear to me, there is changeability and separation.*
- *I am the result of my own deed; whatever deed I do, whether good or bad I shall become its heir.*

It is a fact of modern society that youthfulness is regarded as most desirable, while growing old is to be avoided at all costs. Thus we will go to any extent to appear young even when the body is giving in to old age. We even lie about our age.

******

Age of a young lady. A film star was once brought up before a magistrate for drunken driving and she was asked how old she was, she replied, '30 years.'

A few years later, the same film star appeared in court for the similar offence and this time also she gave her age as '30 years.' Now she was appearing before the same magistrate who remembered her. 'How is that?' he demanded 'five years ago you said you were 30 years old and now you say you are still 30.' Not to be outdone, the fading former actress fluttered her false eyelashes and explained, 'Your honour, I have been told many times never to change my testimony in a court of law. I told you once I was 30 and I will never change my word.'

··*·*·*·*

For all men and women wishing to live happily and make the best of their lives without having to lie like the film star above, self-knowledge is the most essential factor. The first step to know the nature of the mind is to control it through systematic mental development or meditation. Mental culture is productive of insight which can light up a person's life. Like a torch, it brightens the winding path in life and enables him to sort out the good from the bad, the right from the wrong and realise the clear light of insight and he will soon get into the correct path. Therefore meditation is to cleanse the mind.

When we meditate, we should check against hallucinations, especially about our spiritual attainment. Such imaginations can appear even to experienced meditators if they are not careful.

******

A meditator's illusion. Once a monk had developed his meditation to a high state of mental absorption *(jhana)*. He was able to project his mental creations as concrete images that other people could see. Because of this, he thought that he had attained the state of Perfection, an Arahanta (Sainthood).

He had a pupil who practised meditation to a higher degree and became an arahant. When he attained this state, he realised that his teacher was unable to develop further because of conceit. But the problem was how to make his teacher realise this fact.

One day he came to his teacher and asked him if he was an arahanta. 'Of course, I am,' said the teacher, 'and to prove it. I can create anything you want with my mind.'

'Create a big elephant,' said the pupil. A big elephant appeared in front of them. 'Now make him charge at you.' said the pupil. The master made the elephant charge at him. Just as the elephant started charging, the teacher got up from his seat and tried to run.

'Wait. If you are an arahanta,' said the pupil, 'You should have no fear, why then did you get up to run?' Then only did the teacher realise that he had not attained arahantahood.

******

Our physical body lasts less than a century at the most and undergoes changes from moment to moment. Our emotions are but a stream of feelings and images; our minds but a stream of thoughts. Our characters change with the years. Within this complex interaction of mind and body, there is no permanent substance which can be regarded as an unchanging self.

Assume there is a pit about 100 feet deep and we put burning charcoal at the bottom. After that we lower a ladder into it and ask some people to go down one by one. Those who start to go down do not complain about the heat until they go down to a depth of 30 to 40 feet. After 40 to 50 feet, they feel a certain amount of heat. When they go further down to 70 or 80 feet and reach nearer to the burning charcoal, they experience the sensation of burning. In the same manner, young people do not experience suffering although the Buddha says life is suffering. But this is a good analogy to explain that as we gain more experience we see the truth about suffering more clearly.

Admittedly, for convenience in our daily lives, we still talk in conventional terms and use words like 'myself' or 'yourself'. It is like saying that the sun is rising, although we all know that in actuality it is the earth that revolves on its axis and goes round the sun.

4

MENTAL ABUSE AND MENTAL HEALTH

It may not be too difficult to do good; it is more difficult to be good. But to maintain a good mental attitude and to do some service to others in the face of accusations, criticism and obstructions is most difficult of all.

The word 'Man' is presumably derived from the Sanskrit word, 'manas', meaning mind. The human race is made up of not only body, but also mind. Equipped with a mind, Man must be capable of thinking since this is the specific function of the mind. It is through the mind, not the body, that human values can be understood, appreciated and followed.

If a person does not use his mind to think rationally as well as humanely he is not worthy of belonging to the human race.

You are born into this world to do some good, not to pass your days in idleness and become a burden to society. Always think of rising higher in goodness and wisdom. Otherwise you abuse the privilege of this high station attained through your merits.

Of all the infinite number of beings in the universe, the human being has climbed the highest in the uphill struggle towards the summit of perfect existence. We are near the summit, and in one lap or two, we may reach it. But even if we cannot make it to the last lap and reach the top in this life, we can nevertheless still travel on a direct, secure route that could bring us to the summit without the risk of falling back to lower forms of life. The last lap is difficult but with determination we can ensure that we reach a stage where there will be no more turning back.

Our most urgent task, therefore, is to ensure that we do not fall below our present plane of existence. For this purpose, we must try to understand the process of life and realize that each one of us is at the helm of our respective careers. We must steer our lives clear of the lower forms of existence, by keeping to the map of Dhamma.

Life in the Modern World

How does life seem to many people? A tread-mill.

For a quarter of a century, they work to acquire the means of livelihood; for another quarter they struggle amidst perpetual anxieties to accumulate some wealth and property; and in the next quarter, they progress towards death without even knowing exactly why they had lived at all.

Many people are so preoccupied with the business of earning a living that they have no time to live. They try to keep up their external appearances but neglect their internal development. Blinded by their senses, they mistake the false for the real. They work hard – even fight, tooth and claw – for wealth, power and position, thinking that they can be 'successful' if they achieve these rewards of life. Here, one writer tries to tell us how we spend our lives:

> 'We live and work and dream,
> Each has his little scheme,
> Sometimes we laugh,
> Sometimes we cry,
> And thus the days go by.'

One of the greatest maladies facing the modern world is too much action. Action, more action, and still more action punctuate the life of man from the cradle to the grave. Seldom can he spend even five minutes in silence to relax.

Today man can travel at twice the speed of sound in supersonic jets. On land, he can travel at an incredible speed in the so-called 'bullet train', and skim over the ocean surface in a hovercraft. In all these spheres of human activities, the trend is to do more in a shorter period of time. He rushes here and there as modern living makes great demands on him. He snatches a hasty meal and dashes off again to join the daily rat race. He leaps into bed, tosses and turns for half the night. Just as he is dropping off to sleep, the alarm clock goes and he is up once again to begin yet another day. For too long, modern man has abused his body and mind. Human nerves just cannot withstand the pace at which he lives today. So, it will only be a matter of time before they give way. Nature never hurries; neither should we.

Modern man is so busy in his working hours that he sometimes talks and even walks in his sleep. This rapid pace in modern man's life is like the constant roar of the machines he invented. The frittering away of his nervous energies and the dissipation of mental resources weaken both his mind and body.

He seems to be enmeshed in all kinds of ideas, views and ideologies, both interesting as well as foolish. He is greatly influenced by the mass-media, like television, cinema, newspapers and magazines, which shape his way of thinking, desires and life style. Human sexuality is exploited to the hilt in the media to persuade him to buy, even the things he does not need. Music, dance and other forms of entertainment which were introduced for his relaxation have today become like drugs, creating more excitement and restlessness in his mind and arousing his animal nature. In the end, he becomes confused and turns away from the path of rectitude and understanding to follow the easier path of overindulgence and sensuality.

Life as a Battlefield

The world itself is a vast battlefield. Everywhere there is fighting, violence and bloodshed. Existence is characterised by constant struggle: molecules against molecules, atoms against atoms, electrons against electrons, men against men, women against women, men against animals, animals against men, spirits against men, men against spirits, men against nature and nature against men. Within one's physical body, there is constant flux and struggle.

Just like the world, the mind itself is a great field in which many battles are fought. Every little incident disturbs the balance of the mind. The mind becomes exceedingly happy when a son is born. At the next moment, it becomes unhappy when the boy falls sick, meets with an accident or is struck with an incurable disease. The mind fluctuates between the two extremes of happiness and sorrow because it is not trained to see the true nature of life. For that reason, the ordinary man will always experience suffering, fear, uncertainty and very little emotional satisfaction in this world of constant flux. But when a person has trained his mind with meditation and sees the nature of things as they really are, his mind is no longer attached to nor tied down by the world. As a result, he frees himself from suffering and the imperfections of the world.

Life is an eternal battle fought along two fronts: one outward, the other inward. The outer line is intellectualism and rationality. If the strength of the first front is exhausted, man withdraws into the second front of his inner feelings and thoughts and seeks to fight from there anew. When the second front is lost as well, he withdraws into himself to nurse his wounds for a while, only to emerge again and fight on another day. However, when he is completely shattered and withdraws into himself, living on his anger, frustration, desires and fantasies for a long period of time, his sanity becomes affected.

An uncontrolled mind is dominated by the unwholesome thoughts of selfishness, greed and attachment to worldly fame, gains and possessions. If these tendencies are not checked, the mind will turn into a devil's workshop, changing human beings into monsters who are prepared to kill and destroy whoever and whatever is in their way.

For the sake of material gain and comfort, modern man does not listen to the voice of nature. He wants too much out of life, and because of that he 'cracks up'. He is made to believe that 'success' means being able to do everything and be 'the best' in all these activities. Of course, this is physically impossible. His mental activities are so preoccupied with his future happiness that he neglects the needs of his physical body and ignores the importance of the present moment for what it is worth. This inability to get our priorities right is one of the main causes of all our frustration, anxiety, fear and insecurity.

So, what is the result of all this? These anxieties and stress manifest themselves as mental ailments and disturbances, collectively known as 'emotional killers'. These negative emotions of fear, worry, insecurity, jealousy, and so on, not only cause suffering to the person concerned, but also to those around him.

In many developed countries it has been found that about two out of every ten persons are suffering from insanity or are in need of psychiatric treatment for one kind of neurosis or another. More and more hospitals and institutions for the mentally sick suffering from various forms of neuroses are being built. There are many more who do not receive any treatment, but are badly in need of help. The rise in the criminal element, which is sometimes equated to mental affliction within these societies, has reached alarming proportions. One of the far-reaching results arising from the research of Freud is the recognition that *people who are compulsive criminals and delinquents are mentally sick, who are more in need of understanding and treatment than corrective punishment.* This attitude to the problem lies in the basis of all progressive social reform and opens up the way for rehabilitation rather than revenge and retribution.

There are certain common methodologies or techniques in mental therapy to treat people who are mentally unbalanced. Initially, the aim is to bring to the surface the mental states that have long been buried. The psychiatrist encourages his patients to talk and reveal those carefully camouflaged thoughts that have long been hidden even from the patient himself. The psychiatrist deliberately refrains from telling the patient what to do, but tries to bring him to that state of mental awareness where he can see for himself his own mistaken attitudes of mind. Thus, in this way a skilled psychiatrist attempts to reveal the secret for every patient the creator of his illness, which in every instance is none other than the patient himself. This unmasking gives the patient an insight into the hidden nature of his problem as well as how it could be overcome.

This approach is similar to the Buddha's *'Do It Yourself'* method, which aims at making us realise the true nature of life, of ourselves and of our problems. By following this gradual method, we will come to recognise that the great problems in this world are caused by our own craving and ignorance. At the same time, we will also practise the way of reducing our mental defilements and eradicating the root of our problems, thereby enabling us to experience spiritual growth and emerge completely liberated from worldly conditioning and suffering.

Towards Mental Health

The destructive mental forces and emotions must be checked and reduced to a manageable level. In this context, relaxation is a necessity, not a luxury. We should reduce or curtail all unnecessary activities, rise early to have more time to dress and talk to the family, and make a habit of spending some time alone to be engaged in some useful activities like reading, contemplation and for physical and mental relaxation.

All of man's ills depend on how well he attempts to cross life's currents. No man can cross the ocean in a sailing boat by defying the winds; instead, he must adjust his sails to the winds. The currents of life are always streaming in one direction. They will never change the course of their flow, just as the sun does not change its direction. Man must adapt himself to this flow of life to find complete harmony within himself and with his environment.

Obey the eternal law of the universe (Dhamma), taught by the Buddha. He who keeps this law lives happily in this world and in the next. It is the duty of every human being to use his mind in the correct way. The human mind should be channelled towards creating a just, equitable and peaceful world. If the mind is allowed to roam at random, it will become undisciplined, distorted and depraved. Most of the suffering in the world is caused by unruly, distorted or depraved minds. The man who is not at peace with himself cannot be at peace with others.

Hatred is an unhealthy attitude which increases more darkness and which obstructs right understanding. Hatred restricts; love releases. Hatred strangles; love enfranchises. Hatred brings remorse;

love brings peace. Hatred agitates; love quietens, stills, calms. Hatred divides; love unites. Hatred hardens; love softens. Hatred hinders; love helps. By realising the value of love, one must eradicate hatred.

Mankind prays for peace, but there can be no peace in the world until the conflicts within man himself are resolved. For this to be accomplished, there is an urgent need to train the mind. One may ask, 'How can we do it?' While this is a logical question, more important is the question, 'Do we want to do it?' If the answer is a clear 'Yes', accompanied by commitment, one can certainly develop the skill to train one's mind.

The Basic Law of The Mind:-

As you See – so you Feel
As you Feel – so you Think
As you Think – so you Will
As you Will – so you Act

PART II

HOW TO OVERCOME
WORRY NOW

5

CONTROLLING ANGER

An angry man opens his mouth and closes his eyes.

An aristocratic rich widow, well known in high society for her benevolence, had a housemaid who was faithful and diligent. One day, out of curiosity, the maid decided to test her mistress to find out if she was honestly good by nature or if it was merely a pretence put on for the sake of appearance in her fortunate high society surroundings.

The following morning, the maid got up from her bed quite late at around mid-day and the mistress chided her for being late. The following day too, the maid repeated her late rising. The mistress, in rage abused the maid and struck her with a stick thus hurting her. News of this incident spread around the neighbourhood and the rich widow lost not only her reputation but also a faithful servant.

Similarly in this modern society, people are kind and modest when their surrounding conditions are good and satisfactory. When conditions change and become unfavourable, they become irritable and angry. Remember the saying *'When others are good, we can also be good. When others are evil, it is easy for us to become evil.'* Anger is an ugly and destructive emotion. All human beings are subject to anger in one form or another in their daily lives. It is a negative emotion which is dormant within us, awaiting to flare up and take control over our lives when the occasion arises.

Anger can be likened to a flash of light which blinds us temporarily and causes us to act unreasonably. Uncontrolled anger can cause us a great deal of harm both physically and emotionally. Like any other human emotion, anger can be brought under control.

The Danger of Anger

Certain creatures by nature are unable to see during daytime, while some others are blind at night. A human being driven to great heights of hatred and bitterness is blind to anything in the true sense, either by day or by night. There is a saying, *'An angry man opens his mouth and closes his eyes.'*

It is said, that an angry man transfers the effects of his anger to himself when he regains his reasoning. Just as the money stored in the bank will reap a dividend, so will the anger stored in the mind reap the returns of bitterness.

Whom or what do we fight with when we are angry? We fight with ourselves, and become, as it were, our worst enemy. We must try to eradicate totally, this dangerous enemy latent in our minds with a proper understanding of the situation.

Anger grows stronger when fueled by emotion, especially when craving is behind that emotion. At the moment of intense anger, a person ceases to be human: he becomes a dangerous animal capable of destroying not only others, but also himself. Anger can cost him his reputation, job, friends, loved ones, peace of mind, health and even his very own self.

The Buddha spoke about the wretchedness of anger and said that when a person is angry, seven things befall him that would help the cause of his enemies and make them rejoice. What are the seven?

- *He will be ugly despite being well-groomed and well-dressed.*
- *He will lie in pain, even if he sleeps on a soft and comfortable couch.*
- *He will do things which give rise to his harm and suffering by mistaking bad for good and good for bad, by being reckless and not listening to reason.*

- *He will lose his hard-earned wealth and even run into trouble with the law.*
- *He will lose his reputation and fame which have been acquired by diligence.*
- *His friends, relatives and kin will avoid him and stay away from him.*
- *After death he will be reborn in an unfavourable state of existence, since a person who is controlled by anger performs unwholesome actions through body, speech and mind which bring unfavourable results.*

~ *Anguttara Nikaya* ~

These above misfortunes are those which one's enemy would like to wish for one. But these are the very misfortunes that befall a person who is overcome by anger.

Controlling Anger

A good way to control anger is to act as if the undesirable thoughts do not exist in our mind. By using our will-power, we focus our minds on something wholesome and thus subdue negative emotions. It is not easy to react peacefully to someone who insults us. Although the physical body is not harmed, the ego feels humiliated, thereby making a person feel like hitting back. It is not so easy to reciprocate insults with courtesy and respect. But the test of character is how we deal with trying situations that confront us in our daily lives. It seems, even from our childhood, we like to take revenge for our own satisfaction.

'He abused me, he beat me, he defeated me, he robbed me. In him who harbours such thoughts hatred will not cease.'

~ *The Buddha* ~

Darkness cannot be dispelled by darkness but by brightness. In the same way hatred cannot be overcome by hatred but by loving kindness.

Some persons are like letters carved on a rock; they easily give way to anger and retain their angry thoughts for a long time. Some men are like letters written in sand; they give way to anger also, but the angry thoughts quickly pass away. Some men are like letters written in the water; they do not retain their passing thoughts, but the perfect ones are like letters written in the wind; they let abuse and uncomfortable gossip pass by unnoticed. Their minds are always pure and undisturbed.

Even if we feel angry at injustice done to others, we should contain our anger because we are not in a position to arrive at a correct course of action in a disturbed state of mind. When we are angry, we must be aware of our own anger. Observe the anger as a mental state, without directing it to the object that causes the anger. We must train ourselves to observe and analyse our emotions when we are angry. By constantly practising self-analysis of our moods, we will

gain greater confidence in being able to control ourselves and will not act foolishly or irrationally. The
Buddha's advice is:

> *Good is restraint in deed; good is restraint in speech;*
> *good is restraint in mind; good is restraint in every-*
> *thing. The noble man practises restraint all points is*
> *freed from sorrow.*

Not all people adopt the same strategy to control
their anger. One effective way is to employ the 'time-
delay' method. Thomas Jefferson summed up this
approach when he said, *'When angry, count to ten*
before you speak; if very angry, count to a hundred.'
A recipe to develop better control of our temper is
to repeat these ideas mentally several times a day to
ourselves.

> *'I can control my anger,*
> *I can subdue irritability,*
> *I will keep cool and be unruffled,*
> *I will be unmoved by anger as a rock,*
> *I am courageous and full of hope.'*

By repeating these lines, we can strengthen our
minds to gain confidence and mental calmness. When
faced with the thoughtless actions of people, we can
also keep in mind what the Buddha taught:
> *'If a man foolishly does me wrong, I will return to*
> *him the protection of my infinite love; the more evil*

comes from him, the more good shall go from me; the fragrance of goodness always comes to me, and he gains only a bad reputation.'

'A wicked man who reproaches a virtuous one is like a person who looks up and spits at heaven; the spittle soils not the heaven, but comes back and defiles his own person. The slanderer is like one who flings dust at another when the wind is contrary; the dust returns on him who threw it. The virtuous man cannot be hurt; the misery comes back on the slanderer.'

******

Wise persons never challenge foolish ones. A wild boar once decided to become the king of the jungle. So he got up from the dung heap where he was resting and went to the lion, the king of beasts and challenged him to a fight. Of course the lion just turned his nose at the smelly creature, ignoring him and walked away without even bothering to reply. This story illustrates that when wise beings are challenged by those who have a low mentality, the noble ones should not waste their time on them.

******

The Buddha has also given some advice for controlling anger. This advice if followed, grows in effectiveness the more it is practised:

- *By recollecting the advice of the Buddha who*

spoke about the danger of anger and the problems created by harbouring these unwholesome thoughts.

- By recalling some of the good qualities of the hated person. When you disregard his bad characteristics as a human weakness, and start thinking of his qualities and the good things he had performed, then the anger may soften and give way to loving kindness.

- By remembering the ownership of kamma. All beings are the owners and heirs of their respective kamma, and they will inherit the fruits of their good or bad actions. By understanding this law, you will be less inclined to be angry with another. Instead of being angry, you develop compassion for the other person who will have to face the results of his bad actions.

- By cultivating thoughts of loving kindness to all beings. Great blessings come to those who develop their minds through the practice of boundless love and compassion to all.

- By not letting your mind be polluted by evil thoughts towards the person who has wronged or hurt you. The anger you harbour in your mind does you more damage than to the other person. Therefore, cultivate a life of joy and love, even while living among the hateful.

6

THE DANGER OF
SELFISHNESS

Selfishness kills one's personality and spiritual growth.

A self-centred and selfish person lives only for himself. He does not know how to love and respect others; he argues and quarrels over small matters, and his life becomes but an endless journey in unhappiness. He suspects others of being his rivals, and is envious of their success and achievements. He covets their possessions; he cannot tolerate their happiness. In the end, he poisons his thoughts and becomes dangerous to society.

Regardless of whether he is rich or poor, a selfish man is controlled by greed. He is never contented, never satisfied with what he has. It was Mahatma Gandhi who once said, *'The world is enough for everyone's needs, but not ever enough for one man's greed'*. If he is rich, he worries about his house, property and all his other possessions. He always thinks of how to make more money and is not prepared to part with a little of what he has, even for a worthy cause. He is always filled with worries of being robbed, kidnapped, or cheated. He worries about his business and doubts the trustworthiness of his workers. He worries about his death and how his wealth will be used. If he is poor, on the other hand, he suffers from not having enough. He is always longing for wealth and property. When he is unable to obtain the wealth and property through honest means and hard work, he resorts to criminal means to meet his desires.

Selfishness is brought about by wrong views and the failure to perceive the realities of life. Rooted in craving, and the belief in a non-existent self, selfishness is a very destructive emotional force. If preventive and corrective measures are not taken to reduce this negative emotion, it can cause untold suffering and misery. How many of us ever pondered deeply over the statement made by William Gladstone:

'Selfishness is the greatest curse of the human race'

Thoughts are forces, and selfishness is a powerful negative force that brings bad consequences. This is in accordance with the universal moral law that we reap the results of our actions which take root in our thoughts. Pain and suffering are the results of evil thoughts, while happiness is the result of good thoughts.

We are dominated by our thoughts. A chronic hatred or even a cherished grudge tears the one who harbours it to shreds. A strong feeling of resentment is just as likely as a germ to cause poor health and sicknesses. If one is so unfortunate as to have an enemy, allowing the resentment to dig in and the hatred to become chronic is the worst thing one can do to oneself.

The Need to Cultivate Love and Compassion

All living beings are comrades in suffering, who are subjected to a common predicament. In the average human mind, there is a rubbish heap of evil; but fortunately, there is also a storehouse of virtue waiting to be tapped. The choice of developing virtue or committing evil is really up to oneself. The practice of sympathetic feelings for the suffering of others should be cultivated. A happy, contented life is only attained by overcoming selfishness and developing goodwill, understanding and benevolence. We should not condemn others by picking on their weaknesses or mistakes and disregarding their good work and good nature.

In the Dhammapada, the Buddha says: *'Hatred is never appeased by hatred in this world. It is appeased by love. This is an eternal law.'* This natural law was also taught by Jesus who said that *a person should do good to those who hate him.*

To do good is to bring to oneself all the powerful good elements in nature. To do evil is to welcome destructive elements. Those who live in hate will die in hate, just as those who live by the sword will die by the sword. Every evil thought is as if it were a sword directed at him who draws it. Once a person realises this fact, he should be afraid of harbouring evil and selfish thoughts.

It is a spiritual truth that evil can only be overcome by its opposite, positive force of good. Love and compassion are the antidotes for hatred. Goodwill is the antidote for anger. The presence of one positive force implies the absence of its opposing negative force. By developing love, compassion and goodwill, we can make these thoughts our most precious assets.

Nothing outside us can possibly affect us as much as what is taking place in our minds. It is an established fact that, 'As a man thinketh in his heart, so he is.'

Self-conquest is indeed far greater than the conquest of all other folk; neither a god nor a spirit nor Mara, with Brahma can win back the victory of such a person who is self-subdued, and even lives in restraint.

~ *Dhammapada* ~

7

OVERCOMING JEALOUSY AND SELFISHNESS

Selfishness is the cause of jealousy, while jealousy nurtures selfishness.

Once the tail and the head of a snake quarrelled as to which should be the leader. The tail said to the head: 'You are always taking the lead; it is not fair. You ought to let me lead sometimes.' The head answered: 'That cannot be because it is the law of our nature that I should be the head. I cannot change places with you.'

The quarrel went on for several days until one day, out of anger, the tail fastened itself to a tree. The head could not proceed and decided to let the tail have its own way. Unfortunately, the tail was unable to see where it was going, and the snake fell into a pit of fire and perished.

There are some who are never satisfied with their possessions and are jealous of those who have more than they. The jealous thoughts they harbour in their minds prevent them from enjoying what they have. Even if they have done very well in everyone's eyes, they are not satisfied and are tormented by the fact that someone else has performed better than them. It would be beneficial for them to turn their thoughts inwards and count their blessings rather than cultivating jealous thoughts.

The Cause of Jealousy

The basic cause of jealousy is selfishness. When a man becomes eccentric and self-centered, he lives only for himself and regards all other beings as his potential rivals. He is envious of their success. He covets their possessions. He cannot tolerate their happiness. He is jealous of their achievements. In the final analysis, he becomes completely unsociable and dangerous, which create problems. Problems can come from many sources.

※※※※※※

More Troubles Come from Our Kind. A dog took a trip to see the country. A few days later he returned, and his friends asked him whether he faced problems on the trip. He said that he met with many people and

animals along the way. They did not create any disturbances but allowed him to go his own way.

'The only problems I faced were from our own
kind.' he said. 'They would not leave me alone. They
barked at me and chased and tried to bite me.'

******

In the same way, when a person becomes successful, those who do not know him will leave him alone.
Unfortunately, he has to put up with some of his
friends and relatives who may feel envious of his
success. They carry tales, and even create obstacles for
him. In such a situation, he should try to exercise
patience. It may be useful for him to remember that it
is easier for some people to associate with strangers
rather than their own people.

Selfishness is brought about by wrong views and
failure to perceive the realities of life. Selfishness is a
very destructive emotion based on craving and causes
untold suffering and misery. Corrective and preventive measures should be taken to control such negative
emotions.

Thoughts are forces in which good builds upon and
attracts good. The fruits that we reap are in accordance with the thoughts we have sown. Our pain and
happiness are direct results of our own evil or good
thoughts on the basis of the law of attraction which
operates universally on every plan of action. If one is
so unfortunate as to have an enemy, the worst thing
one can do to oneself, and not to the enemy, is to let

the resentment dig in and allow the hatred to become chronic.

We are all comrades in suffering and subjected to a common law. The choice to develop virtue or commit evil lies with us. Therefore, if we cannot bear to see or hear the successful achievements of others, we would need to re-evaluate our outlook.

Awareness of the Mind

By reviewing and examining one's negative thoughts, a person will realise that no one outside himself has the power or means to upset his inner peace and balance of mind. When he compares himself with others, he creates his own suffering by thinking that he has less or that others are more successful than him. There is no benefit to be gained by harbouring jealousy, which is often the cause of so much disunity in the world.

We should realise that negative emotions such as jealousy, anger and ill-will stifle the mind's growth. We must work to free ourselves from such evil influences at all costs. Jealousy will not bring us what we desire, but instead will lead us down the blind alley of enmity, unrest, and undue physical and mental suffering.

We must be ever vigilant of unwholesome thoughts. Whenever a negative thought arises in the mind, we must try to replace or substitute the negative thought with a positive one. This requires us to be aware of what goes in and comes out of the mind.

Through this gradual process of self-awareness, we will be able to check and weed out the negative thoughts before they can enslave us.

Dealing with Jealousy

When we come to know the danger of harbouring jealousy, we can then devote our time and energy to the profitable cultivation of wholesome thoughts of kindness and sympathy. We should think that there is nothing for us to lose when others make progress. We should cultivate modesty, eradicate self-centered craving, and develop sympathetic joy at the happiness of others. A person who is imbued with such good thoughts is a blessing to himself and the world at large. The practice of sympathetic feeling for the sufferings of others should be encouraged while at the same time eradicating thoughts of selfishness. A happy and contented life is only attained when one overcomes selfishness and develops goodwill, understanding and benevolence.

The Buddha encouraged his disciples to develop sympathetic or appreciative joy when others are happy, which is an effective antidote to jealousy. They adopt a congratulatory attitude by rejoicing when others prosper and succeed. This may not be hard to do when our loved ones prosper and succeed, but is rather difficult with regard to our adversaries. Just think: 'Do we not want to prosper and succeed? Do we not wish to be blessed with happiness? Just as what we would want for ourselves, wouldn't the others too want to be blessed with prosperity, success and happiness?' Maintaining such a mental attitude can free a person from much suffering as well as from falling to ruin, especially when ill-will and malicious actions develop from jealous thoughts. It also prevents one from hindering others in making good progress.

On the other hand, we must have patience with others who are jealous of our success. Their reaction can sometimes arise because we have not acted with humility . We must be considerate by not flaunting our achievements before others who are less successful. During moments of success, we must recall our past failures so that we may understand better the feelings of others who have performed less well.

When others act against us because of jealousy, guard ourselves against resentment. We should remind ourselves that we, like others, are owners of our respective deeds (kamma). We should think thus: 'Now what is the point of my getting angry with him? Anger will not solve problems, they will only aggravate the situation. This anger will only create kamma which will lead to my own suffering and downfall. By replying to him with resentment, I will only hurt myself like a person who picks burning embers in his hand to hit another with it.' There is a story which clearly illustrates how a Dhamma master subdued a jealous rival without resorting to anger.

******

Can you make me obey you? Once there was a Dhamma master whose talks were widely attended by people of all ranks. He never used scholastic explanations but spoke straight from his heart to his listeners.

One evening, a teacher from another religious sect attended his talk. He was angry because this Dhamma master was able to draw large audiences, including some of his own followers. The self-centered teacher was determined to have a debate with the master.

'Hey, Dhamma Master!' he called out. 'Wait a minute. Others may listen to you and obey what you say, but a man like myself does not respect you. Can you make me obey you?'

'Come here beside me and I will show you,' said the Dhamma master.

The teacher pushed himself through the crowd and proudly stood beside the master.

The Dhamma master smiled. 'Come over to my left side.' The teacher obeyed.

'No, I think it's better if you are on my right side,' said the Dhamma master. 'We can talk better that way.' The teacher proudly stepped over to the right.

'You see,' said the Dhamma master, 'you are obeying me. I think you are a very gentle person. Now sit down and listen.'

******

8

DEALING WITH ENEMIES AND CRITICISM

'Lord, save me from my friends. I know how to defend myself against my enemies.'

~ *Voltaire* ~

Very few people can claim they have no enemies. Even great religious teachers who had so selflessly served mankind, like the Buddha, Krishna, Jesus and Mohammed, great philosophers like Socrates, social reformers like Abraham Lincoln and the father of non-violence, Mahatma Gandhi, all had their share of opponents and enemies. These great masters and leaders patiently underwent the abuses and criticisms of their enemies, without deviating from their noble principles. Some even had to face untimely death for the sake of their principles which they valued above everything else.

Ever so often, people who work for the welfare of others also come into contact with people with bad intentions. There seems to be a continuous conflict that arises naturally between good and evil. When a person makes an effort to do some good, there are some people who like to find fault with him rather than shower him with praises. He is blamed for what he does or doesn't do. In addressing Athula, a disciple of the Buddha, who complained about his dissatisfaction with the preaching of other disciples, and of the way they tried to answer his questions, the Buddha said: 'People blame others for their silence. They also blame those who talk much or in moderation. There is, therefore, no one in this world who is not blamed.'

A person must be prepared to accept blame with some degree of resignation if necessary, even if the allegations are without basis. Abraham Lincoln had a very sober and practical way to handle criticism. He said, *'If I were to try and read, much less answer, all the attacks made on me, this shop might as well be closed for any other business. I do the very best I know how, the very best way I can; and I mean to keep on doing so until the end. If the end brings me out all right, then what is said against me won't matter. If the end brings me out wrong, then ten angels swearing I was right would make no difference.'*

Mirror of the Mind

A person's thoughts and beliefs shape his life, experiences and circumstances. Like mirrors, all men become like their own reflected mental images. They behold the reflection of their own character and inner thoughts. Until a person realizes that his own character is but the effect of his own thoughts and beliefs, he remains a victim of circumstances. But once he realises this great truth, he has started on the journey which will enable him to be free from the poison of ill will.

The ugliness a person sees in others is a direct reflection of his own nature. Therefore, a person should not act hastily and project the image of unwholesomeness and hatred within himself on another innocent and unfortunate being. Let us have patience and not criticise others too readily. We should view things from a broader perspective by putting ourselves in the other person's shoes. Try to understand the circumstances which gave rise to an action. Adopting such a perspective can enable us to lead a noble life of non-interference in the affairs and the peace of others. Let us keep in mind the Buddha's advice: *'He who is observant of others' faults, and is always irritable, increases his own defilements. He is far from the destruction of defilement.'* Boltan Hall has written the following lines:

'I looked at my brother with the microscope of criticism,
And I said, 'How coarse my brother is!'

I looked at him through the telescope of scorn,
And I said, 'How small my brother is!'
Then I looked in the mirror of truth,
And I said, 'How like me my brother is!'

Picking Faults in Others

It is so easy to see the faults of others: it is difficult to see one's own faults. The Buddha says that one winnows other's faults like chaff, but hides one's own like a crafty fowler who covers himself. One should not regard the faults of others, things done or left undone by others (just to pass remarks,) but one should constantly consider one's own deeds of commission and omission.

Keeping these gems of advice in mind can help us understand better our own nature and put a brake on negative mental tendencies. Be positive. If one has a fault-finding frame of mind, one will see that even a rose has its thorns. But why dwell on the flaws when one can enjoy its beauty? Every worldling has faults. And it is useful to remember that no person is totally bad, or evil either.

The next time before we start finding faults with others, remember these lines by Robert Louis Stevenson:

'There is so much good in the worst of us,
And so much bad in the best of us,
That it will not behove any one of us,
To find any fault with the rest of us.'

What to do when Criticised

When someone is angry with you, try to find out the cause of the problem. It could be due to something which you have done. If you have made a mistake, admit it and apologise for your wrong action. If it is due to a misunderstanding, have a heart to heart talk with that person and be willing to resolve the differences. On the other hand, if the anger has arisen because of jealousy or emotional problems on the part of the other party, you should not reply anger with anger, though this is a natural tendency. Wars do not end wars. They only give rise to more vengeance. At best, they result in an unjust settlement. The Buddha says, *'The victor breeds hatred and the defeated lives in misery. Only he who renounces both victory and defeat is happy and peaceful.'*

Overcome anger with loving kindness. This is by no means easy to perform. And this implies some degree of self control: to conquer your own anger for the sake of happiness and peace. The Buddha says, *'Though one should conquer a thousand times a thousand men in battle, he who conquers his own self, is the greatest of all conquerors.'* It takes patience, but the results are worth the effort.

Smile and do so sincerely. As you smile and shower benevolent thoughts of love and kindness upon an enemy, a miracle happens. Your radiant face and presence generate positive mental waves that can break the cold mental wall separating the both of you. Only love has the power of influencing and changing negative thoughts into positive ones: hatred will only succeed in hardening an opponent's position.

> *He drew a circle that shut me out*
> *Heretic, rebel, a thing to flout.*
> *But love and I had the wit to win:*
> *We drew a circle that took him in!*
>
> ~ *Edwin Markham* ~

The wise do not get rid of their enemies by returning evil for evil since more enemies are created that way. The proper method to overcome your enemies is by extending to them your goodwill and understanding. Recognise their needs and why they attacked you. Then, instead of criticising, speak well of them. This is not what most people do, but it works time and again. It was Oscar Wilde who once said, '*Always forgive your enemies, nothing annoys them so much*'. The experiences of people who use this method clearly demonstrate that this is a most effective, practical method of changing an enemy into a friend. This is also the Buddhist way.

The Buddha taught that *one should conquer anger with kindness, wickedness with goodness, selfishness with charity, and falsehood with truthfulness.*

Before we get angry with someone whom we consider to be an enemy, just recall two things: Firstly, people suffer more from the hatred they carry in their minds than what their enemies would do to them. If you wish to be rid of your greatest enemy, remove your own anger.

Secondly, we not only learn from our good friends, but from our enemies as well. We must give them the benefit of the doubt. They could well be **right.** If we don't pay attention to **what** they say (instead of being angry with **how** they say it), we might lose an opportunity to learn and improve ourselves. Sometimes, this revelation might be something of importance, but because it is so close to us even our own friends might hesitate to point that weakness to us. If we keep an open mind, without coming to hasty conclusions, we can learn much from our enemies.

Don't Be Afraid of Criticism

Sweetness can cause sickness. Praise is sweet, but too much of it can cause one to be sick. Criticism can be like a bitter pill or a painful injection: It is unpleasant surely, but it can do us good.

Don't be afraid of criticism. Remember that no one can really be free from it, not even great people. Critisism is futile because it puts a man on the defensive and usually makes a man strive to defend himself. Critisism is dangerous because it wounds a man's precious pride, hurts his sense of importance and arouses his resentment. But there is a constructive side to criticism. We should listen to criticism, especially if they are constructive, and welcome the opportunity for self improvement. We should restrain our ego and not harbour hatred against the critic. We must not be quick to label those who do not share our views as our enemies. Not all who criticise us are our enemies. Therefore, adopt a positive attitude and listen intently to the message of the criticism. Does it have a basis and is there something we can learn from it? We may find out our own weakness which we might not be able to see.

On the other hand, we may come across some incorrigible people who are not affected by our goodwill. We may try by using peaceful methods and reason with them, but it will be in vain. Even then we should not harbour anger and take revenge against them. Because by doing so, we will fall into the same pool of mud they are wallowing in. Getting involved in mud-slinging will make us no better than our enemy. We defile ourselves in the process. Many people interfere with unnecessary things either to do something malicious or to pass uncalled for remarks. As a result of this negative attitude, they get into trouble.

At the same time we should not be too critical or inquisitive about other people's affairs and poke our noses where we are not wanted. There is an Eastern folk tale to illustrate this point.

******

Mind your own business. Once, some woodcutters were cutting a fallen tree trunk. They began by splitting the trunk down the middle. To make their work easier they inserted a wedge between the two parts as they proceeded. As it was almost noon they decided to take a break, leaving the tree trunk with the wedge still in place. Just then a monkey came along. He wanted to know what the wedge was doing there. So he sat astride the trunk, with his tail (and other organs!) hanging between the split trunk. After shaking the wedge vigorously, he succeeded in removing it, but in so doing the two sides of the trunk slammed shut crushing his tail and his other organs and killing him.

******

What should you do when someone makes an unkind statement? You may like to reflect: *Is my enemy justified in his actions and statements?* If they are completely baseless, then instead of getting upset you should ignore them. You may even have compassion because the person who acts out of ill-will only succeeds in harming himself. If you are innocent, regard your enemies as ignorant and in need of guidance. Remember Jesus who said, *'Father, forgive them for they know not what they do,'* when he was crucified.

One of the best ways to avoid such problems is to reduce as much as possible contact with such evil people. This is why the Buddha once said that *if you do not have any reliable friends to associate with, it might be better to lead a solitary life.*

This may not always be possible. What should we

do if we have to associate with selfish friends who try to take something from us? They are like mosquitoes, not only do they suck our blood, they can also spread viruses. In that case, seek ways to reduce any reason for instigation. As the Dhammapada saying goes, '*Let us live happily amongst those who hate*'. On no account should we allow ourselves to be drawn into revenge, which might often seems to be a sweet option. Try to rise above petty troubles. We are angry because our ego is hurt. If we can remove the false view of ego, then we can realise that there is really nothing to be angry about and there is no one at whom this anger is directed.

While developing patience and understanding, we must not, however, allow ourselves to be made use of by others for their own gain. We should maintain a calm dignity in the face of unjust attacks, but at the same time, we should not surrender our noble principles.

※※※※※※

You may step on my feet. While walking down the corridor in the compartment of a train, a young man accidentally stepped on the foot of a fellow passenger. Even after apologising, the young man was scolded by the angry man.

'My dear fellow,' said the young man, 'can't you see that this was an accident? If you are still not happy with my apologies, you may step on my foot if you like.'

This brought some sense to the passenger who felt ashamed of himself for what he had done to the young man and he stopped scolding him immediately.

******

Some people may be inclined to think that some of the above illustrations are very commendable, even noble, but impossible to accomplish and impractical in this uncaring world of ours where survival of the fittest is the order of the day. Granted it is difficult, but certainly it is not impossible. Although people take delight in committing evil, within their nature lies the potential to overcome evil and attain complete liberation. A person commits evil for immediate gain, but for his future gain he should perform what is good. Ever so often, one's impatience for immediate results blinds him from setting his sights further and higher. When he adopts a broader vision, even if he cannot return good for evil, at least he should take care not to return evil for evil, much less evil for good.

You should not give up your good work just because of criticisms. If your principles are honourable and if you have the courage to carry on despite criticisms, you are indeed great and can succeed anywhere.

Those who devote their time and do some service to others gain appreciation and criticism as well. Some are jealous of them. This is a natural worldly condition just as the tree that bears sweet and edible fruits gets more pelting from the people.

The Buddha says, *'The noble swerve not from the right path, and crave no longer after worldly joys, let happen what may. The wise remain calm and constant in mind, alike in joy and in sorrow.'*

Do not expect to see immediate results the very first time you attempt radiating loving kindness towards your enemy. And do not be disheartened if you are not rewarded for your efforts. You must have confidence, determination and perseverance to carry on this practice to win over your enemies. By so doing, you give your enemy the opportunity to realise that he has erred. He will come to appreciate your gentleness and courage.

In trying to win a friendship or to end a quarrel, you should not say that you are in the wrong, when that is not the case. If you have made a mistake, admit it freely and humbly. However, if you are right, stick to your principles, but maintain a pure heart – a heart free from anger, hatred and vengeance. On the other hand you should not try to look down upon small people or minority communities, by considering them as powerless. There is a saying that *a great man shows his greatness by the way he treats little men.*

Even humble creatures can topple any giant beast if they co-operate.

******

Unity is strength. An elephant once pulled a branch off a tree where there was a bird's nest. As a result the nest and the eggs in it were destroyed. The bird was very upset but the elephant just walked off without even saying he was sorry. The bird flew to the woodpecker for help and the latter sought out the elephant and plucked out his eyes. Swams of flies then settled on the elephant's eye sockets and infected them. Blinded, the once mighty elephant wandered about helplessly looking for water. The bird, still seeking vengeance, asked some frogs to get into a big dry hole and croak from there. The elephant, thinking there was water, rushed to the hole, fell into it and was killed. So the bird, woodpecker, flies and frogs, all humble creatures together could destroy a powerful animal like the elephant. Minority groups can similarly change the destiny of the world if only they speak out with one voice.

******

9

GAINING CONTROL OVER MOODS

Moods can create an unpleasant atmosphere in society besides exposing an ugly face.

Everyone is influenced by moods to some extent. We should try to understand our moods better so as to gain control over them and to avoid doing things we might regret later. When under emotional stress, we should defer making important decisions. When we are angry or in a bad mood, we cannot see or think clearly to come to good, well-considered decisions. At the other extreme, when we are elated and flushed with happiness, we tend to be more accommodating and less objective in our thinking.

Any decisions reached during such periods are likely to be biased. Take some moments to allow the mind to calm down. Analyse the problems. Think them over. Decisions or judgements made with a calm mind uninfluenced by moods will be less biased and better.

Changes in moods are reflected on our faces. Verify this by looking at a mirror. It is incidentally a good way of curing ourselves of our ever changing moods. It makes us want to laugh when we see how silly we look with a scowl or sulky expression. On the other hand, when we smile and relax the facial muscles, it has the effect of uplifting our spirits and making us happy.

Our changing moods also show how transient mental states are. In all these changes, the 'ego' which people take to be permanent is only illusory, like mere shadows. When we are happy, sad or angry, we say 'I am happy, sad or angry'. However, this is merely a conventional way of referring to oneself. But where is this I which feels these moods? Is it in the head, the heart, the 'soul'? If we analyse ourselves carefully, we will see that there is really no permanent 'I' but a series of mental and physical energies which die as quickly as they rise. Zen master Dogen said: *'To study Buddhism is to study yourself, to study yourself is to forget yourself and to forget yourself is to perceive yourself as all things.'*

If there really was a permanent 'I', it would always appear the same, without change. We would never grow old. It is because these mental energies rise and

fall so rapidly that we seem to think of them as continuous and permanent. We find it hard to think otherwise, just as it is so hard to believe that actually it is
the earth that goes round the sun. If we can see the
reality of ourselves as non-existent, then we can see all
our emotions – good and bad – as merely hindrances
along the path to the attainment of peace and harmony. Such an understanding can provide a handle to
control our moods better.

Imagine our body as being a motor bus and all these
moods as passengers. They are trying to get in the
driver's seat to take control of the steering wheel.
What do you think will happen in such a situation?
An accident or a crash will result. And this is what
happens to most people in their lives, if they do not
know how to handle their changing moods which
cause their character to be rather unstable.

You must reduce the number of passengers. Drop
some off at the bus stops along the way. Get rid of
those who are troublesome. Get rid of your anger,
greed, worry, jealousy, ill-will and so on which influence your moods. With such harmful distractions
out of the way, there will be no jostling for the
driver's seat and you will be able to drive in peace.
You will be in full control of the bus. Your body and
mind will be under your control and you can go
where you want to. You will be the master of yourself.

This conception of 'Self' causes a lot of trouble.
Because we think we have a permanent self or ego, we

attach undue importance to ourselves. We get into the habit of thinking that our needs are more important over everyone else's. When we see those better than we are, we jealously put them down. When we see a rich man, for example, we do not feel happy for him (as we should) but try to dig into his past to expose whatever skeletons he may have in his cupboard. Again, if others are better looking than ourselves or are more skilled at doing something, we become envious. The best way to combat these negative feelings is to develop *sympathetic joy* in the success of others. Try to unload the pride or superiority complex we carry with us in our minds, we earn more friends otherwise we invite problems.

The lack of sympathetic joy creates another failing. We are unwilling to acknowledge the help we receive from others on which we build our own success. We like to think we did it all by ourselves. Good friends are often lost when people do not know how to appreciate them for their kindnesses. There are many successful people in the world today who even refuse to acknowledge the help given to them by their parents. Ingratitude such as this must be eradicated at all costs.

Consideration and Kindness

When in a bad mood, people are sometimes cruel or ill-mannered towards those less fortunate than themselves. They assume a false sense of superiority. ' *I call no man charitable,' said a writer, 'who forgets that his barber, cook and postman are made of the same human clay as himself.'* When we fail to be kind to all men, we destroy our own peace of mind. The jewelled pivot on which our lives must turn is the realization that every person we meet during the day is a dignified member of the human race.

Whether our acts of consideration for others be large or small, the principle is the same. Those who treat an employee with tact and diplomacy will go a long way to make him happy. A happy, motivated employee is of great value to any organisation. The need to be considerate to other beings – human or animal – can best be illustrated by a story.

******

Do not rush into anything. Once, a king was learning the art of charioteering from a master horseman. As soon as his chariot arrived at an open field, the king started to use the whip in a race with his teacher, even before his horse had a chance to warm up. Very soon he fell behind the master horseman and could not catch up with him no matter how hard he tried. This made the king furious. He summoned the master horseman: 'It appears you have not taught me the best skills in driving a chariot!'

'Your Majesty,' the master horseman replied, 'I taught you all the skills of driving a chariot, but you have overused them. We charioteers have a rule: we must first take into consideration the horse's total condition and then act in accordance with it. When you fell behind, you became so anxious that you whipped the horse madly without any concern for its well-being. Your Majesty, you only cared about being first and had no concern for your horse. That is why you fell behind.'

******

Acting Out of Compassion to All

'*Seek not happiness other than by being worthy of it. Seek happiness in the joy of duty which is nobly done,*' taught the Buddha. Here is a fundamental basis of the art of social interaction. Here is a moral teaching of human fellowship, not of abstract faith. Here is a concept of personal growth and the creation of happiness in any society.

Sometimes people act out of anger and hatred even when they are not influenced by moods. The history of the human race would have been different, if kindness and consideration had been practised at all times. However, throughout history, man is seen to have been more interested in inflicting suffering than in alleviating it. This is a strange fact which is difficult to understand. Look around for ourselves. Albert Einstein said, '*The world is too dangerous to live in, not because of people who do evil but because of people who sit and let it happen.*'

Due to man's foolishness and ignorance, he cannot fathom the pain he inflicts on others. Poor and help-

less animals are being tortured or killed by the so-
called civilised men in their pursuit of sport and
adventure. The poor and innocent are callously exploited to gratify and satisfy the cravings of modern
society. So many have to suffer and die for the entertainment and pleasure of a few.

It is bad enough to strike at a defenceless animal or
to exploit another human being, but to laugh and take
delight at such inhuman activities is to reveal the
weaker and darker side of the human personality.
Foolish people take delight in committing evil with a
false sense of pleasure. Pain is a common experience of
all that live. We all feel pain. Yet in our midst, there
are some who can laugh at the pain suffered by others.
It is not funny when someone hurts himself. It is also
not funny to see anybody suffer. Unfortunately,
many do not seem to think that way. To be noble,
people must renounce these defiled mental states.
They must learn to develop compassion and a caring
heart for the welfare of all creatures, great and small.

10

THE PRESSURE AND PLEASURE OF BRINGING UP CHILDREN

If we have not expressed our gratitude to others for their services, how can we expect our children to show their gratitude to us?

The family is the oldest social unit in this world. It is, in fact, a society in miniature. And it is the duty of each generation to pass on the torch of civilisation to the next.

Most parents love and cherish their children. There is no sacrifice a loving parent is not prepared to make for the well-being and happiness of his children. Unfortunately, modern materialistic influences and pressures have now made the burden of parenthood greater than ever before. It even threatens to tear the family apart, the most fundamental social structure which had been formed by the human race before the dawn of civilization.

Pressure on Parents

There are many causes for this. First of all, the economic pattern during the last two hundred years has changed drastically from agriculture to industry. No longer does the family operate as an economic unit on the farm. The parents work away from their children who are generally referred to as 'latch-key' children and only return home after office hours. The nature of their work requires them to be time conscious and they are rewarded according to their work performance. During a time of recession, they are exposed to the insecurity of either being laid off or getting a reduction in pay.

Children are exposed to a wide range of expectations, consumption patterns and demands by their peers in school or other activities featured in advertisements through the mass media which parents are being pressured to meet. In addition, parents are sometimes being evaluated by critical children who are better educated than themselves. They may not even have very much in common with their children to strike a simple conversation. This rift between parents and children is known as the generation gap.

These changes place great pressure on parents, many of whom seem unable to cope with the psychological demands. Besides all these, the two world wars of this century have created frightening experiences which many have gone through and which have caused whole nations to change their views about a benevolent God who cares for all the creatures he made. In this age of science and technology, such concepts propagated by many religions have been found to contradict mankind's own experiences and modern scientific discoveries.

Pressure on Children

Most parents have their worldly expectations and will feel a sense of failure or inadequacy if their children do not live up to them. Great emphasis is placed on materialistic attainment and scoring points before their friends and neighbours, while spiritual values are sadly neglected. Unfortunately, their children fall victim to these psychological pressures. They are encouraged to excel in their studies, to secure jobs that pay well, to climb up the social ladder, and to accumulate as much wealth as possible. Many parents do not place too much value on virtues such as gratitude, honesty, integrity, kindness, consideration and tolerance. The pursuit of wealth and worldly success are far more important to them.

Due to such social pressures, parents, either rightly or wrongly, and without thinking of the consequences, encourage and even force their children to work hard and compete for the so-called 'success'.

They impose their value systems on their children who are under pressure to be smart, to be popular and to excel. They are under the impression that success means the ability to compete, conquer and quell opposition, ignoring the need to establish an inner harmony with oneself.

Whether the children have the interest or not, they are expected to attend classes on computers, music, ballet, swimming, and so on, under the misguided belief that such activities are very important for success and happiness. There is nothing wrong in pursuing such healthy activities if the children are interested, have the required talents, or if they are meant to enrich their child's awareness of themselves and the world around. The cultural activities and accomplishments are necessary to make a human being more cultured. A richer understanding of the beauty of life should help children become more understanding, more compassionate, and appreciative of the beauty of nature around them.

It is natural for parents to see their own features and characteristics reflected in their children.

******

My beauty and your brain. George Bernard Shaw was once approached by a seductive young actress who cooed him in his ear:- 'Wouldn't it be wonderful if we got married and had a child with my beauty and your brains?' George Bernard Shaw who was hardly a handsome man replied: 'My dear, that would be wonderful indeed, but what if our child had my beauty and your brains?' The actress who did not need much persuasion just sped off.

******

It is important to differentiate between what is necessary and what is not. Success and happiness do not lie in mastering such accomplishments alone. Parents should not place the children under such pressure – to be brilliant beyond their capabilities, to be leaders when they are not ready for leadership, or to be star athletes when they have no sporting attributes. As a result of unrealistic goals, children are prematurely forced into a world of adult pressures and responsibilities. The outcome: they are always tired and listless. They are not able to enjoy the carefree life of childhood. These pressures have also the undesirable consequence of giving rise to emotional insecurity in their adulthood. Let us not transfer our ambitions to them and rob them of their childhood.

Recognising Potentials

A parent should be aware of the potential within his child – of what he can accomplish in the future in his own way and in his own good time. Children are not mature enough to plan for the distant future. You cannot expect a primary school student to set his sights on going to university, deciding his career, or about his marriage. But one thing is certain. There is no such thing as a 'useless child.' Every human being has some talent, some potential. An academically 'stupid' child may be born 'natural' in motor mechanics or cooking. It is, therefore, the duty of parents to recognise what a child is good in, his aptitudes, to pay particular attention to such gifts or talents, and encourage the child to develop them for the good of society and the child's sense of fulfilment. Try to train the children according to their mentality to do something which they can do for their living.

******

A powerful formula for recital. In one of the Jataka stories (previous birth stories of the Buddha) there is an amusing story. Once upon a time the Bodhisatta or Buddha-to-be was a well known teacher who used to impart his knowledge by giving instruction for higher studies, since the proper institutes of higher learning were rare at that time. Intellectual teachers used to accommodate a few students at a time and taught them art, languages and some other important subjects. They concentrated more on moral discipline, religious knowledge and also taught them how to live harmlessly as good citizens as they were very concerned about the careers of their students. The Bodhisatta teacher observed that one of the students in his class was weak in his studies and this had bothered him very much. Instead of applying pressure, he devised a way to enable the weak student to earn his own living.

One day the teacher called this pupil of his and

kindly told him that his education was good enough and that the time was ripe for him to concentrate on his household life in earning a livelihood. Accordingly, the Bodhisatta teacher taught him a very powerful secret formula to recite when needed. The pupil was elated about the kind gesture of his teacher. He then bade him farewell and left with all hopes and confidence for the future. Taking heed of what he had learnt, he concentrated more on the formula given to him by the teacher rather than doing any other work. The words of this formula however gave different meanings according to prevailing circumstances.

One night, as he was sleeping outside his house, he heard noises of some one digging the ground nearby. In surprise, he woke up and commenced to recite the formula. The meaning of the recital was *'Digging and digging, why are you digging.'* Hearing this voice, the people who were digging discarded their tools and ran away in fear. On hearing this commotion, he got up and went to investigate what had really happened. To his surprise, he saw a box of gold coins. The thieves apparently had buried the box after their robbery the previous night and were trying to retrieve their stolen goods, when they got frightened on hearing the recital and fled. The young man was lucky to have recovered the gold coins. The King having heard that this young man had a powerful formula which when recited could chase away robbers, invited him to sleep near the palace gate.

One day, as he was sleeping near the palace gate, he

was suddenly awakened by the sound of someone digging. Immediately he started to recite his formula. *'Digging and digging, why are you digging?'* On hearing this, the thieves who were trying to rob the palace by breaking through the palace walls gave up their digging and ran away. Hearing this commotion, the gate keepers and the guards in the palace chased after the robbers and caught them. They realised that the reciting of the formula by the young man had helped them to catch the thieves. When the king came to know about this incident, he invited the young man into his palace and appointed him as one of his close attendants.

The young man being elated, was very happy and dutifully attended to his duties diligently. The king having heard of the power of his formula requested the young man to teach it to him. The king committed it to memory and recited it whenever he was free. On one of such occasion, there was a plot being hatched to assassinate the king in order to usurp his throne. The commander in chief of the army had requested the barber to cut the king's throat while shaving the latter's beard and promised to give the barber a big reward. The next day, the barber as usual arrived with the shaving kit to shave the king's beard and started to sharpen the razor in preparation for cutting the king's throat as directed by the commander. While the barber was using the stone to sharpen the razor, the king coincidentally started to recite the formula which meant: *'Rubbing and rubbing, I know why you are rubbing'*. The barber got a shock and fainted. The king was however not aware of the plot to assassinate him and so asked the barber what the matter was and what had happened to him. To the king's surprise, the barber revealed the secret and how he had been asked to cut the throat of the king by the commander in chief. Immediately the king summoned his cabinet and passed the death sentence on his commander in chief and the young man who taught him the secret recital was made the commander in chief in place of him.

******

If teachers and parents try to understand the mental capacity, the intrinsic mental habits and the potential talents of their children, there will be no difficulty in training them to be good citizens.

Parents must re-evaluate their priorities. It has become fashionable for parents to compare the academic achievements of their children with other parents. By all means encourage the child to excel in his studies, but a child should not be evaluated only on the basis of his academic achievement. We must accept him for what he is, and not what we expect him to be. Yet, this is what all parents are unconsciously guilty of. All this does not mean parents should allow their children to grow up without training or to aim for excellence. They should be encouraged to excel, after taking into account their aptitudes, inclinations, and abilities. Human beings are not all born equal, so parents must recognise their children's potentials and help them to excel in those areas in which their potential is strong.

Parents should try to recognise the natural ability of their children instead of imposing their ideas on them. Not all children are born to be engineers and doctors. Yet, when given every encouragement and support, their aptitudes will develop and they can grow to their fullest potential.

******

Child prodigy. Once a boy who was gifted in poetry was born into a poor family. He would spontaneously speak in verses even when conversing with others. His talent impressed many people but not his father, who being uneducated, was not able to appreciate his son's talent. One day when his son replied to him in poetry, he became very angry and started beating the boy. While he was being caned, he replied to his father in poetry.

> *'Dear father, please,*
> *Cane me if you must;*
> *But poetry is the gift I was born with,*
> *It's a gift I did not ask for*
> *Nor is it one that I could lose;*
> *Allow me, dear father, to use it at least.'*

******

Parents should ensure that their children be given a good education, and also be equipped with a strong ethical and moral code of conduct. It is only with good ethical and spiritual training that a child can grow to realise his true potential. Francis Story, the learned Buddhist writer, says:-

Knowledge is needed for success in the world,
Meditation is needed to realise Nibbanic bliss;
Sila (morality) is necessary for both.

Parents have to teach and guide their children not only by precept but also by example. Teach them how to fulfil their duties and responsibilities and to show their gratitude to elders and parents. It is by example that children learn and remember best.

******

Bring back the basket. Once there was a young couple who lived with the husband's father. This old man was very troublesome as he was always bad tempered and never stopped complaining. Finally the couple decided to get rid of him. The man put his father in a large basket which he slung over his shoulder. As he was preparing to leave the house the man's son, a little boy aged ten asked, 'Father, where are you taking grandfather?' The man explained that he was going to leave him for a while out in the mountains to fend for himself. The boy kept silent as he watched his father walking away and suddenly he shouted, 'Father, don't forget to bring the basket back.' Surprised, the man stopped and asked the boy why? The boy replied, 'Well, I'll need the basket to carry you away when you are old yourself.' The man then quickly brought his father back to the house and ever since took care of him well and attended to all his father's needs.

******

There are some narrow minded parents who commit certain immoral things and use vulgar words at home.

Parents must take special care when they are going to do something in the presence of their children.

The following poem on raising children offers some practical points on the art of raising children.

If a child lives with tolerance
he learns to be patient.
If a child lives with encouragement
he learns confidence.
If a child lives with praise
he learns to appreciate.
If a child lives with fairness
he learns justice.
If a child lives with security
he learns to have faith.
If a child lives with approval
he learns to like himself.
If a child lives with acceptance and friendship
he learns to find love in the world.

Many carefree parents allow their children to behave as they wish without imparting them any moral guidance. It is questionable whether parents can succeed in teaching their children after they reach adulthood when it is too late. Instead of day dreaming all the day long positive action should be given in teaching them love, respect, harmony and above all to be citizens of the world.

One source of worry for parents is the thought that their children are not very obedient or filial. They worry that their children will not care for them when they are old. They also fear that their children will bring them shame and unhappiness through their misbehaviour thus spoiling the good name of the family. As a rule, parental love is greater than filial love. One cannot expect immature and inexperienced children to be as dutiful and loving as their parents. Until and unless they themselves become parents, only then will they realise the value of parents and their love.

There are cases where parents have given their best to educate their children and teach them good values, but these efforts have all been thrown to the wind due to the stubborn and rebellious nature of their children. There are some incorrigible children, born to the best of parents. In such event, parents need not be remorseful as they have already done their parental duties expected of them. Parents should develop an understanding to change what they can and to accept what they cannot.

Khalil Gibran has written a few meaningful lines for parents to contemplate, as to who your children are:

Your children are not your children.
They are the sons and daughters of life's
longing for itself.
'They come through you but not from you.
And though they are with you yet they
belong not to you.
You may give them your love
but not your thoughts,
For they have their own thoughts.
You may strive to be like them, but seek not to
make them like you.'

The Buddha had the same thing said in the Dhammapada. A person with limited wisdom may think that his children and wealth belong to him. But even he himself is not his own, what more to speak of children and wealth. How can he believe that he owns them when he cannot control or prevent the changes that his children and wealth will have to undergo.

Some parents place demands on their married children, who have their own problems, and are themselves under tremendous pressure in society. When parents complain about their children's ingratitude it only succeeds in keeping them away due to guilt and shame. But if parents develop the virtue of equanimity, they will remain calm and not make undue demands on their children. This will bring a greater sense of closeness and understanding between parents and children and create the desired oneness in the family.

Parents in Modern Society

One of the saddest things about modern society is the lack of parental love which children in highly industrialised countries suffer from. When a couple gets married, they usually plan to have a number of children. And once the child is born, parents are morally obliged to care for him to the best of their ability. Parents are responsible to see that a child is not only satisfied materially; the spiritual and psychological aspects are very important too.

The provision of material comfort is of secondary importance when compared to the provision of parental love and attention. We know of many parents from the not-so-well-to-do families who have brought up their children well with plenty of love. On the other hand many rich families have provided every material comfort for their children but have deprived them of parental love. Such children will grow up devoid of any psychological and moral development.

Read **'Parents And Children'** by Narada Thera (BMS Publication) for a more detailed treatment of the subject.

11

THE FEAR OF DEATH

'Life is uncertain, death is certain.'

~ The Buddha ~

'The world is afraid of death; to me it brings bliss.'

~ Guru Nanak ~

Once life is launched, like a bullet it must reach its destination, which is death. All of us have to face this inevitable, natural phenomenon whether we like it or not. The sooner this truth is accepted, the better we will be able to direct our lives for a good purpose. Actually, we are disturbed not so much by death itself, but by the wrong view we hold of it. Death in itself is not that terrible; what is terrible is the fear of death that prevails in the mind.

Our life-span is controlled by our biological clocks which are continuously ticking away. When they run out, sooner or later, there is little we can do to gain extra time. Once our time is up, we must be prepared to go through the natural process of death.

A veteran nurse once said, 'It has always seemed to me a major tragedy that so many people go through life haunted by the fear of death – only to find when it finally comes that it is as natural as life itself. For few are afraid to die when they get to the very end. In all my experience, only one seemed to feel any terror – a woman who had done her sister a wrong which was too late to set right.'

'Something strange and beautiful happens to men and women when they come to the end of the road. All fear, all horror disappears. I have often watched a look of happy wonder dawn in their eyes when they realise this is true. It is all part of the goodness of Nature.'

As the famous physician, Sir William Oslet puts it, 'In my wide clinical experience, most human beings die really without pain or fear.'

Coming to Terms with Death

All human beings, irrespective of sex, or race, creed, will have to come to terms with death. There is no alternative escape. Death is an inevitable process of this world. It is not often that we are brave enough to come face to face with the thought of our own mortality. Yet, man is not free in life unless he is also free from the fear of death.

To be afraid of dying is like being afraid of discarding an old worn-out garment.

~ Gandhi ~

It is hard to bear the loss of people whom we love because of our attachment to them. This happened to Visakha a well-known lady devotee during the time of the Buddha. When she lost her beloved grand-daughter she visited the Buddha to seek advice in her sorrow.

'Visakha, would you like to have as many sons and grandsons as there are children in this town?' asked the Buddha. 'Yes, Sir, I would indeed!'
'But how many children die daily in this town?'
'Several, Sir. The town is never free from children dying, Sir.'

'Then, Visakha, in such a case would you cry for all of them? Visakha, those who have a hundred things beloved, they have a hundred sorrows. He who has nothing beloved, has no sorrow. Such persons are free from sorrow.'

When we develop attachment, we also must be

prepared to pay the price of sorrow when separation takes place.

The love of life can sometimes develop a morbid fear of death. We will not take any risks even for a rightful cause. We live in fear that an illness or accident will put an end to our seemingly precious permanent worldly life. Realising that death is a certainty, we hope and pray for the survival of the soul in heaven for our own security and preservation. Such beliefs are based on strong craving for continued existence.

According to psychological studies, much mental stress is caused by our refusal to face facts and accept life's realities. This stress, if not overcome can eventually lead to grave physical illness. Certainly worry and despair over illness will make it worse. We cannot pick and choose the kind of illness we desire, nor can we choose the suitable or auspicious time to die. But we can certainly choose to face illness and death without fear.

People are frightened of dead bodies, but in the true sense the living are in fact far more dangerous than dead bodies. Dead bodies do not harm us, but the living are capable of doing enormous harm and could even resort to murder. So is it not a foolish belief, for people to be afraid or frightened of dead bodies?

What is Birth and Death?

Man need not have to fear death. Birth and death are like two ends of the same string. You cannot remove one end while wishing to keep the other. The mystery of birth and death is very simple. The coming together of mind and matter – also known as the five aggregates – is called birth. The existence of these aggregates is called life. The dissolution of these aggregates is called death. And the recombination of these aggregates is called rebirth, and so that cycle will go on repeatedly until such time as we attain the blissful state of Nibbana.

There are many ways to interpret this simple and natural occurrence called 'DEATH'. Some believe that death means the complete dissolution of a being without a hereafter; some others believe in the transmigration of a 'soul' from one body to another; and to others it means indefinite suspension of the soul, waiting for the day of judgment. To Buddhists however, death is nothing more than a temporary end of this transient phenomenon. It is not the end of this so-called 'being'.

Each and every individual should be aware of the role of death in his or her destiny. Whether royalty or commoner, rich or poor, strong or weak, a man's final resting place within this life is either in a coffin lying buried six feet underground or in an urn or strewn over the sea.

All human beings face and share the same fate. Due to ignorance of the true nature of life, we often weep and wail and sometimes even smile and weep again. When once we realise the true nature of life, we can face the impermanence of all component things and seek liberation. Until and unless we achieve our liberation from worldly conditions, we will have to face death over and over again. And in this respect, too, the role of death is very clear. If a person finds death to be unbearable, then he should make every endeavour to overcome this cycle of birth and death.

Peaceful Death

Everyone hopes and desires to have a peaceful death after having fulfilled his lifetime duties and obligations. But how many have actually prepared themselves for such an eventuality? How many for instance have taken the trouble to fulfil their obligations to their families, loved ones, friends, country, religion and their own destiny? It will be difficult for them to die peacefully if they have not fulfilled any of these obligations.

We should first and foremost learn to overcome the fear of death which not only humans but also gods are subjected to. Let not the present moment escape us. Those who have allowed fleeting time to pass away frivolously will have good cause to lament when they face themselves nearing the end of their lives.

If people depart from this world without fulfilling their obligations, whatever they may be, their birth as humans in this existence would be in vain as it had been neither beneficial to themselves nor to this world. Therefore, we should not neglect our duties and thus prepare ourselves to face death bravely and peacefully. And one day, we will be able to attain the ideal deathless state where we will be free from all suffering.

It is important to realise that we are born to this world to do some service for the weal and happiness of mankind. We will be remembered by humanity more for what we have done for mankind than what we have done for ourselves. The Buddha says, 'Man's body will turn to dust, but his influence and services remain.' This can be seen in the tangible achievements of the exemplary works of great men which still remain with us to this day, helping to shape our way of life even though they are no more living among us. In a sense, we could regard them as still being with us as a testimony of their valuable services rendered to mankind.

When people see their own lives as being only a drop in an ever-flowing river, they will be moved to contribute their little part to the great stream of life. The wise know intuitively that to live they have to work for their liberation by avoiding evil, doing good and purifying their mind.

People who understand life according to the Teachings of the Buddha never worry about death.

******

I died today. David Morris was a well known Western Buddhist scholar who died at the age of 85. Soon after his death this present writer received a letter from him (obviously he had written it earlier with instructions for it to be posted on his death.) It went like this, 'You will be happy to know that I died today. There are two reasons for this. Firstly, you will be relieved to know that my suffering from the sickness has finally ended. And secondly, since I became a Buddhist I have faithfully observed the five precepts. As a result you know that my next life cannot be a miserable one'.

******

According to Buddhism, death is not the end of life but the beginning of another life within Samsara. If you do good, you can have a better future life. On the other hand, if you do not wish to be reborn again, you will have to eradicate the craving for existence and other defilements from your mind.

Death is Inevitable

It is rather paradoxical that although we so often see death taking toll of lives, we seldom pause to reflect that we too can soon be similar victims of death. With our inate strong attachment to life, we are disinclined to carry with us the morbid thought, although a reality, that death is a certainty. We prefer to put this awful thought as far away as possible – deluding ourselves that death is a far away phenomena, not to be worried about. We should be courageous enough to face facts. We must be prepared to face reality. Death is a factual happening. Death is a reality.

12

WHY WORRY ABOUT THE FUTURE!

'Look to this day. In its brief course lie all the verities of existence – Action, love, transience. Yesterday is but a dream, and tomorrow veiled. Live Now!'

The Buddha was asked this question: Why do the noble beings who have developed their minds appear so calm and radiant? The Buddha replied:

'They sorrow not for what is past,
They yearn not after that which is not come,
The present is sufficient for them:
Hence it is they appear so radiant.
By having longing for the future,

By sorrowing over what is past,
By this fools are withered up
As a cut-down tender reed.'

We Do Not Worry About Our Future

People are often worried about their future. A fortune teller who visited a temple questioned the monk, 'Reverend, would you like to know about your future?' The monk knew what he was up to and replied, *'As monks, we do not worry about our future.'*

The fortune teller then saw two girls at the type-writer and asked them the same question. They had previously overheard the monk's reply and so told him that they too did not have to worry about their future. Since the man could not get anyone to listen to his fortune telling, he decided to leave the temple. As he left, the monk remarked, 'It seems that you, too, have missed a chance to gain something for your own future.'

The secret of happy, successful living lies in doing what needs to be done now. We should not worry about the past and the future. We cannot go back into the past to undo the things we have done. Nor can we anticipate everything that may happen in the future due to conditions in the world which are constantly changing and unpredictable. There is but one moment of time over which we have some conscious control – 'the present!'

This Truth has always been recognised by all the great thinkers in this world of ours. They saw that it is futile to live with memories of the past and with dreams of the future, neglecting the present moment and its opportunities. Time moves on. Let us not stand idly by and see our hopes for success turn into memories of failures. It lies within our power to build something today. The Buddha has shown us the way to maintain cheerfulness through contentment. The time is now and the choice is ours.

Kalidasa, a great Indian poet and playwright wrote the following lines in Sanskrit on the simple truth of living in the present:

'For yesterday is but a dream,
And tomorrow only a vision,
But today, well-lived, makes every yesterday
A dream of happiness,
And every tomorrow
A vision of hope and joy.
Look well then to this day.'

Worrying About the Future

Many people worry when thinking about their future. There is no reason for people to worry if they have learned to adjust themselves according to the circumstances of their daily life. In addition, they should also take advantage of what is possible at present. The ability to shape the course of one's life can only be exercised in the present, not the past or future. Only in the present can one stop or start doing a thing. Whatever castles he builds in the air and whatever dreams he has in his mind will come to naught if he does nothing about it.

He who is subservient to the future becomes the plaything of fortune. Some people are in the habit of consulting fortune-tellers and astrologers when faced with worries or difficulties. While there are some astrologers who can make good predictions, there are a large number of unscrupulous men out to make a fast buck by pretending to know how to foretell the future. People who go to such fortune tellers are sub-consciously masochistic and love hearing that the future holds misery for them. Fortune tellers are quick to assess the personalities of their clients and generously oblige them with terrifying tales of the bad luck that will befall them. These gullible people spend their money on rituals and so-called charms and amulets to avoid the misfortunes. On the other hand, when they are told that some good luck will come their way, they spend large sums of money to win at gambling or lotteries. In either case, 'A fool and his money are soon parted'.

Changing One's Fortune

People worry unnecessarily over their health, family, income, fame and possessions. They try to maintain stability in that which is inherently unstable. The more they worry about their future, the more they lose their confidence in their lives and develop selfish desires. He who is constantly trying to change his condition in life knows no peace of mind.

A sufferer who believes in fate will think, 'This was preordained, this was allotted to me by God; therefore I must pray to God and ask him to correct my way of life'. He may spend more time for praying to the extent of neglecting his day to day duties.

If we believe in Kamma, we will reason as follows, 'This is the result of my own activities in previous lives or in this life itself. I must try to rectify the balance by making the effort in doing good and by strengthening the mind through meditation. In doing so, the unfavourable effect of certain kammic forces can be subdued and he can gain success.

> 'There are no stars which we could trust,
> There is no guiding light,
> And we know that we must
> Be good, be just, be right.'

> 'Do not hark back to things that have passed,
> And cherish the future not yet come.
> But who with vision clear can see,
> The present which is here and now,
> Such a wise one should aspire to win,
> What never can be lost nor shaken.'

Instead of worrying unnecessarily about the future, do what can be done now in making fuller use of your potential. Remember, the present is the child of the past, and the parent of the future.

PART III

INGREDIENTS FOR HAPPINESS

13

HOW TO FIND REAL HAPPINESS

'Happiness,' said Life, 'is a wayward prize,
To be won by men with patient striving;
Half the race you have run, now please arise,
And push on, the goal is at the turning.'

Do you want happiness? This simple question will always be answered with a big 'Yes'. Yes, we all, without exception, want to have happiness, although the idea of what constitutes happiness and how it can be obtained differs from person to person.

One writer says, 'Happiness, as viewed by most people, is a much sought for destination. It is something to be. It is something to become. To this unfortunate lot, happiness is the end of the rainbow, the pot of gold. They spend a lifetime chasing rainbows. They might as well chase their own shadows for they shall never find in the external that which only resides within.'

Happiness is in the journey, not in the destination. *Happy is he who has lofty and noble aspirations. Happy is he who is enriching the lives of all those about him. Happy is he who allows others to live peacefully without disturbing them. Happy is he who is contributing something to make this world a better place in which to live. Happy is he whose work, whose chores, whose daily tasks are labours of love. Happy is he who loves love. Happy is he who is happy.*

All men crave for happiness. They work hard day and night to gain happiness, even if it is known to be fleeting. Yet, despite their striving, they are often further rather than nearer to what they have tried so hard to work for. Why is this so?

The Search for Happiness

Modern life is a struggle – a struggle to gain monetary rewards, comfort and luxury. Instead of bringing happiness, this lifestyle brings anxieties and stress. There are important moments in everyone's life when all material things are of little value when compared to the mental or spiritual joy of detachment from worldly things.

In living a lay life, the importance of economic

welfare for leading a good life cannot be understated. We should not pretend that people can be happy if they are starving and living under miserable conditions. Poverty and living in slum areas can stifle human happiness. It is a wretched life in the slums if a large family has to live, eat, sleep and procreate in one small hut. The wretchedness of the environment and the desperate lives of the residents therein can often make such areas a breeding place for vice and bitterness – unless it comprises a community of saints who seek peace in poverty.

However, it is useful to remember that wealth and poverty, happiness and misery, are all relative terms. One person may be rich but unhappy; another may be poor but happy. Wealth is a blessing if rightly and wisely used. But part of the tragedy of the poor is their selfish desire for material things. If their cravings are not fulfilled, they live with resentment. The tragedy of the rich is their inability to rise above their wealth. They cling to their wealth foolishly. Hence happiness is not found in either case, with the poor or the rich.

Some people think that a good and congenial life partner is a source of happiness. It may be so to some extent. Other people think that children are another source of happiness. But these are not stable conditions either. A life partner can die or leave them, while some children could bring more sorrow than happiness to their parents.

We should learn to be contented and happy with

what little we have which has been bestowed on us. We should even be happy and contented with our present state of being even though we are not fortunate enough to be blessed with the least of our humble expectations.

******

A childless wife. There was once a poor childless couple. Although in all other respects they were happy, the wife had a very strong maternal instinct and she desperately wanted to have a child of her own. The husband suggested that they adopt one but she wouldn't hear of it saying that it must be her own flesh and blood. They tried all sorts of remedies but nothing seemed to work. The wife became more and more depressed and the stress, anxiety and sense of inadequacy, became overpowering and began to affect her mental health. Gradually however the husband began to notice a change in her. She pretended to be pregnant, when in fact she was not. Then, one day when he returned home, he found her radiantly happy, cuddling a little bundle. He examined the bundle and found it was nothing more than a little block of wood. She cherished it most dearly showering it with all her motherly love as if it were a real baby. She went through the motions of caring for her 'baby', dressing it up as a mother would do. She even made a cosy cot and rocked her 'baby' to sleep while she sang a soft lullaby. In fact she began to behave very much like a child playing with a doll. The husband became very worried about his wife's condition, and he took her to consult a well known psychiatrist. Now this expert studied her case carefully and made a startling, though very human decision. He explained to the husband that the woman had finally found happiness by imagining what she could not get in reality. He advised that depriving her of that happiness would be far more cruel than trying to get her to behave 'rationally' and throw away the block of wood.

******

We see here that sometimes our decisions regarding other people must be guided by the heart rather than the cold intellect. We could also mention in passing that if we crave for anything beyond reason it can affect us mentally and upset our sense of balance.

Congenial conditions in one's political, economic and social environment are important for one's happiness in a society. Sir Philip Gibbs in his book, Ways of Escape, says, 'What human nature is trying to find, in its eternal quest for happiness, is some system of government and society which will give to every individual a full and fair chance of developing his personality to the utmost: by interesting work and not too much of it; by security for himself and his family and his fellow humans; a sensitive and generous-hearted man cannot be happy if masses of human beings are suffering around him; by a decent minimum of comfort, and by liberty of thought and action restricted only by a code of honour which forbids him to be hurtful to his neighbours. In that liberty of thought and action he has his chance of adventure and delight: of becoming aware of beauty, penetrating further into knowledge, getting more mastery over himself and his surroundings, reaching out to everything in life which is worth having for mind and body.'

Buddhism teaches to adopt harmless and righteous means to gain happiness. There is no meaning in trying to enjoy one's happiness by causing suffering to another person or other living beings. This is in keeping with the advice of the Buddha: *'Blessed are they who earn their livelihood without harming others.'*

Ingredients for Happiness

In building a happy, purposeful life, we should exercise our compassion and wisdom, the two wings that can fly man to the summit of human perfection. If we are to develop the emotional aspect neglecting the intellectual, we will become good-hearted fools, while the development of our intellectual side at the neglect of the emotional will make us hard-hearted intellectuals with no feelings for others. According to the Buddha, compassion and wisdom must be developed jointly for man to gain liberation. Good life is inspired by love and guided by knowledge.

What is compassion? Compassion is love, charity, kindness and tolerance. It is acting out of love and concern for all that live, especially when they are in unfortunate circumstances.

And what is wisdom? Wisdom is seeing things as they are, and acting out the noble qualities of the mind. When a man sees a beautiful woman and is attracted to her, he wishes to see her again and again. He derives pleasure and satisfaction from her presence. However, when the situation changes and he can no longer see her, he must not act unreasonably and behave foolishly. This unsatisfactory side is a fact of human experience. If he has no unrealistic attachment or selfish clinging to her, he will be relatively free from that suffering. In the pleasures of life, there are pains and sorrows. While there is no denying the happiness that people derive from sense pleasure, the nature of such pleasure is brief and does not offer lasting happiness. The realization of this fact is wisdom.

The ingredients for happiness are simple. Happiness is a state of mind. It cannot be found in the material things about us, such as wealth, power or fame. Those who spend a lifetime harvesting and accumulating more wealth than they need will be disillusioned and disappointed when they discover, only too late, that all the money in the world cannot buy a grain of happiness. The search for pleasure must not be confused with the search for happiness. Pleasure is a passing show and does not offer lasting happiness. Pleasure can be bought, but not happiness.

Happiness comes from within, based on the foundation of simple goodness and clear conscience.

No one is happy unless he is contented with himself. The quest for mental tranquillity is only possible through mental culture or meditation. There is so much to do, and so little is done. Only through self-analysis and purification will our latent seeds of virtues be able to sprout to reveal our divine and human nature. It is not an easy task. It requires perseverance, determination and effort.

Happiness is a perfume you cannot pour on others without getting a few drops on yourself.

If you want to live peacefully and happily, allow others also to live peacefully and happily. Unless and until you adjust yourself to live according to these noble principles you cannot expect happiness and peace in this world. And you should not expect gratitude from others. Dale Carnegie says, 'If we want to find happiness, let us stop thinking about gratitude or ingratitude and give for the inner joy of giving. Ingratitude is natural, like weeds. Gratitude is like a rose. It has to be fed, watered, cultivated, loved and protected. '

It is not in man's nature to appreciate anything that comes to him easily. However when these things are taken away then only does he appreciate it. The air we breathe and our vital organs are all taken for granted and we even abuse them, sometimes until it is too late.

We should not be like a fish which does not know the value of water until it is taken out of it.

'It has been my observation, says Abraham Lincoln, 'that people are just about as happy as they make up their minds to be.'

You cannot hope to gain happiness and peace by simply praying. You have to work to gain such blessings. Belief in God and praying for blessing for protection is useful but you should not forget to lock the door when you go out from the house. Because there is no guarantee that God will look after your house until you come back. You should not neglect your responsibilities. If you act according to moral principles, you can create your own heaven right here on earth. But when you violate them, you can feel the hell-fire on this earth itself. People wring their hands and grumble when they do not know how to live according to the natural and cosmic law of kamma and create a lot of their own troubles. If each man tries to lead a respectable life as a gentleman, we can all enjoy real heavenly bliss in this world, without waiting to die to enjoy it. There is no need to create a heaven elsewhere to reward virtue or a hell to punish vice. Virtue and vice have inevitable reactions in this world itself. One of the most baffling questions mankind is faced with is whether there are places called 'heaven' and 'hell' in existence. People have no clear understanding on this concept.

******

Where is heaven and hell? There was once a monk whose favourite subject for his preaching was 'heaven and hell'. One of the devotees who was getting tired of listening to the monk's constant repetition, one day stood up and asked: 'Tell me where is this heaven and hell? If you cannot answer me, I will call you a liar!' The monk being an innocent person became afraid. Instead of answering he kept silent. His silence made the man even more angry and he shouted: 'Speak to me or I'll beat you up!' The monk quickly gathered his wits and replied, 'Hell is around you now, with your anger.' The man, realising the truth, calmed down and began to laugh. He then asked: 'Where is heaven then?' to which the monk replied: 'It is now around you, with your laughter.' Heaven and hell are what we make of our lives. Heavens and hells exist in any part of the universe where living beings exist. There are no such separate places.

******

Where is Happiness?

Where do we look for happiness? 'Within you,' says the Buddha. Nobody will deny that happiness is the most desirable state of being. Happiness is not something which simply happens. Happiness is a state of consciousness that does not depend upon the physical appetites and passions.

✻✻✻✻✻✻

The contented man who had no shirt. A certain Oriental king who was very unhappy sought the advice of a philosopher. The philosopher advised the king to search for the most happy and contented man in his kingdom and to wear his shirt. After a long search the King finally found the man – but he had no shirt!

✻✻✻✻✻✻

A Well-known writer says: *[referring to the Buddha] If you want to see the most contented and happy man in this world, look at the prince in the beggar's clothing.*

Unsatisfied desire is the main cause of unhappiness. Get rid of your desires, and you will be free from your unhappiness. *'One thing only do I teach,'* says the Buddha, *'the cause of suffering and the way of cessation from suffering. Just as sea water has one taste, so is my teaching which deals with suffering and its cessation. I will show you the path from the unreal to the real, from darkness to light, and from death to eternity.'*

Peace or satisfaction is also dependent on one's needs. Dogs like bones but not grass. Cows like grass but not bones. In the same way, some people like excitement more than peace; for others peace is more important than excitement. Just as delicious food to one man can become harmful to another; the medicine which cures the sickness of one can become the cause of death to another. One person's pleasure can become a nuisance to another.

Happiness is a mental state which can be attained through the culture of the mind. External sources such as wealth, fame, social position and popularity are but temporary sources of happiness. They are not the real sources of happiness. The real source is the mind. The mind which is controlled and cultured is the real source of happiness. The opinion that mental tranquillity is unattainable is not true. Everyone can cultivate inner peace and tranquillity through the purification of the mind.

By renouncing that which is perishable on earth, one can get the imperishable gift of happiness.

14

FINDING PEACE AMIDST STRIFE AND CONFLICT

A boil cannot be cured by merely cutting it off. In the same manner, we never experience peace by force but by removing the main cause of the conflict.

Never before in the history of the world, has the human race been in such great need for freedom from conflict, ill-feeling, selfishness, deceit and strife. We are in dire need of peace not only in our homes, offices and in our personal lives, but also at global level. The tension, anxiety and fear arising from conflicts are not only disruptive but constitute a constant drain on our being, mentally and physically. Human beings have become the most violent beings in this world.

Unrest and Global Conflict

Today, the threat of global nuclear destruction is a real possibility. Should there be a global nuclear war, there can be no sanctuary anywhere under the sun for man to escape to. What a mess the human race has landed itself in! Scientific advancement which has made possible the tapping of the tremendous energy within the atom has also endangered the human species. As long as man is dominated by ignorance, selfishness, injustice, vengeance and other kindred evil destructive forces, no one will be safe from him.

It has been recorded that the "blinding flash" of the first atomic bomb on Hiroshima altered the course of world history. The flash which radiated from Hiroshima created suffering, fear, hatred and uncertainty to millions of lives all over the world. In stark contrast, the glorious light that 'flashed and radiated' with the enlightenment of the Buddha under the Bodhi tree more than 2500 years ago was also of great significance to human destiny. It illuminated the way for mankind to cross over from the world of darkness filled with greed, hatred and delusion to a world of light filled with love, kindness and happiness.

The basic problem we face today is moral degeneration and misplaced intelligence. In spite of all the advances made by science and technology, the world is far from being safe and peaceful. Science and technology have indeed made human life more insecure than ever before. If there is no corresponding spiritual improvement in our approach to human problems then human life itself will be in danger.

The Buddha showed mankind the way to a new world of peace, prosperity and goodwill. But today, the human race has ignored this timeless message. Nuclear destruction is just only a button away for man who has gone astray. Man may have gained control over the forces of nature, but he is not in control of his own nature. If he continues in this way, there is only one way he can proceed – along the path to self-destruction and extinction.

In the search for peace and harmony, world leaders have attempted to formulate international treaties and agreements to prevent or settle disputes among nations. The United Nations as a world body was established after the Second World War to maintain international order and stability. It might not be the best vehicle to achieve that purpose but at least it provides a workable system whereby disputing nations can meet in a civilised manner to settle their problems. The hostility, fear and suspicion among different races, nations and religious denominations, however, do not make peaceful co-existence an easily accomplished goal. Despite the endless hours of negotiation and rhetoric at the United Nations, countries are still fighting one another and ceasefire agreements are broken with impunity and predictable regularity. Where do people find peace and happiness under such circumstances? Happiness never arises when there is fear.

Establishment of Peace

A happy and contented life cannot be achieved if we waste our time and energy in conflict and strife. To have peace, we must renounce conflict of every description. The heart, once freed from such strife, will then be free to become the instrument of welfare that it should be, instead of being a hindrance to society. The invisible and powerful mind can be diverted to the weal of mankind, instead of its woe.

A boil cannot be cured by merely cutting it off with a blade. The contaminated blood will only produce more and more boils. The root cause must be investigated first and eliminated to effect a radical cure. Similarly, for there to be peace, the heart and mind, which form the basis of human action, should also be at rest. This can be brought about through a sincere spiritual awakening. What is of importance is not mere faith but for people to lead a life of love, sincerity and justice based on the moral principles taught by religious teachers.

Going Beyond Worldly Pleasures

Religious teachers always maintain that human happiness does not depend upon the satisfaction of physical appetites and passions, or upon the acquisition of material wealth. This fact is also clear from empirical human experience. Even if we have all the worldly pleasures, we cannot still be happy and peaceful if our minds are constantly obsessed with anxiety and hatred, arising from ignorance with regard to the true nature of existence.

Genuine happiness cannot be defined in terms of wealth, power, children, fame or inventions. These are no doubt conducive to some temporary physical comfort but not to happiness in the ultimate sense. This is particularly so when possessions are unjustly obtained or misappropriated. They become a source of pain, guilt and sorrow rather than happiness to the possessors.

Fascinating sights, enchanting music, fragrant scents, delicious tastes and enticing body contacts mislead and deceive us, only to make us slaves of worldly pleasures. While no one will deny that there is momentary happiness in the anticipation of as well as during the gratification of the senses, such pleasures are fleeting. When viewed in retrospection, a person can understand the fleeting and unsatisfactory nature of such pleasures, paving the way to a better understanding of this reality.

If material possessions are the precondition of happiness, then wealth and happiness would be synonymous. Is this a fact? A poet disagrees with this belief thus:

'Can wealth give happiness? Look round and see
What gay distress! What splendid misery!
What fortune lavishly can pour.
The mind annihilates, and calls for more!'

Wealth cannot quench the burning thirst of craving.

We can never be happy if we merely seek to satisfy our gross animal desires, to satisfy our need for the pleasures of food and sex. If it were so, then with the tremendous progress achieved in every field, the world could well be on the road to complete happiness. But this is obviously not the case. Worldly desires can never be entirely satisfied because the moment we obtain something we want, we soon become dissatisfied with it and crave for something else. When the changes and decay occur in the many things we cling to, we experience unhappiness. The enjoyment of sensual pleasure is not real happiness. True happiness can only arise from the full freedom of the mind. The source of happiness is not physical: it must be found in a mind free from mental disturbances.

Worldly treasures are impermanent but transcendental treasures like confidence, morality, generosity, honesty and wisdom are imperishable. Emotional attachment, hatred and jealousy debase a person; but goodwill, sympathetic joy and an unbiased attitude will make him noble, even divine in this life itself.

Man can develop and maintain his inner peace only by turning his thoughts inwards instead of outwards. Be aware of the dangers and pitfalls of the destructive forces of greed, hatred and delusion. Learn to cultivate and sustain the benevolent forces of kindness, love and harmony. The battleground is within us, and it is within us that the greatest battle has to be fought and won. The battle is not fought with weapons, but with mental awareness of all the negative and positive forces within our minds. This awareness is the key to unlock the door from which conflict and strife as well as wholesome thoughts emerge.

The mind is the ultimate source of all happiness and misery. For there to be happiness in the world, the mind of the individual must first be at peace and happy. Individual happiness is conducive to the happiness of the society, while the happiness of society means happiness to the nation. It is on the happiness of nations that the happiness of the world is built.

From the lessons of life, it is clear that real victory is never gained by strife. Success is never achieved by conflict. Happiness is never experienced through ill-feeling. Peace is never achieved by accumulating more wealth or gaining worldly power. Peace is gained by letting go of our selfishness and helping the world with acts of love. Peace in the heart conquers all opposing forces. It also helps us maintain a healthy mind and live a rich and fulfilling life of happiness and contentment.

15

MORALITY: THE SANCTITY AND DIGNITY OF LIFE

*'Observing morality is like putting up a fence to pro-
tect your own house and your neighbour's house
against robbers.'*

Morals and ethics form the core of the social,
economic, political and religious ideals. If love
is the blood of life, then surely morality is its back-
bone. Without virtue life is in danger, but without
love life is dead. The quality of life is enhanced with
the cultivation of virtue, and when virtue arises the
vessel of love overflows. Since man is imperfect by
nature, he has to make an effort to develop virtue.

The cultivation of morality is a very important

aspect of life. Many people have a mistaken idea of what morality is. To them it means the adoption of external modes of behaviour such as dressing, etiquette, artificial and hypocritical manners. They forget that such imitative and conventional morality is man-made, conditioned by society and is, therefore, subject to variation and liable to become out of date. The dressing suitable for one climate, period or civilisation may be out of place, or even indecent in another climate or era. A dress code is entirely a question of custom, and not a deep moral issue. The problem here arises when convention is confused with valid and unchanging universal principles.

Language does make a difference in our thought and actions but it is not all that determines our perception. Food, drinks and religious values all act as perceptual filters; even one's situational values are barriers to truthful cognition.

From these distinctive traditions, problems and aspirations, one set of people have a tendency to believe that only their views are real and that every right thinking person is expected to respect their views as they do. This kind of egoistic idea is very unhealthy. The main determinants of perception and beliefs are past experience, current needs and future expectations.

What is morality? It is the standards and principles of good behaviour in accordance with the path of righteousness. The Pali word for it is *Sila*. It means: self discipline for moral development. It implies a personal discipline developed from within and not arising from the fear of punishment. It is acting out of pure motives – out of love, non-attachment and wisdom, which are strengthened with an understanding of the illusory nature of 'self' and 'ego'.

There is a saying in the Malay language: *'Kesal dahulu, jangan kesal kemudian.'* It means *'Regret beforehand, don't regret afterwards.'*

******

When Socrates met his teacher. During his younger days, Socrates visited a brothel and as he was coming out of it he saw his teacher passing by. The young man was embarrassed and tried to sneak away but the teacher accosted him and asked why he was trying to avoid him. Socrates replied that he was ashamed of what he had done. His teacher advised him, 'You should have been ashamed of your actions before you entered the house of ill repute. Then you would have avoided doing the deed which you are now ashamed of.'

******

Vice is easily learnt without a master,
whereas virtue requires a tutor.
Good habits are difficult to acquire
but easy to live with.
Bad habits are easy to acquire
but difficult to live with.

Morality is the first step in the path towards eternal bliss. It is the basic spiritual foundation. Without this base, there can be no human progress and spiritual advancement. Even worse is a person without virtue for he not only endangers himself but also others around him. After establishing the moral foundation, a person can proceed to develop his mind and wisdom. This practice will lead him from the lower level to the progressively higher levels of mental development, and finally, to the summit of all attainments – Enlightenment.

Mere learning is of no avail without actual practice. According to the Buddha, *the learned man who does not practise the Dhamma is like a colourful flower without scent.* There is a great need for the teaching of virtue by precepts and examples, as shown by the Master himself who served humanity with great compassion. The moral and philosophical teachings of the Buddha are to be studied and practised, and above all, to be realised. Therefore mere book knowledge without common sense and understanding is of no use to overcome our problems.

******

Do not become slaves to any holy book. There was once a man who formed a religious cult and people regarded him as a very learned person. He had a few followers who recorded his instructions in a book. Over the years the book became voluminous with all sorts of instructions recorded therein. The followers were advised not to do anything without first consulting the holy book. Wherever the followers went and whatever they did, they would consult the book which served as the manual in guiding their lives. One day when the leader was crossing a timber bridge, he fell into the river. The followers were with him but none of them knew what to do under the circumstances. So they consulted the book.

'Help! Help!' the Master shouted, 'I can't swim.'

'Please wait a while Master. Please don't get drowned,' they pleaded. 'We are still searching in our holy book. There must be an instruction on what to do if you fell off from a wooden bridge into a river.'

While they were thus turning over the pages of the holy book in order to find out the appropriate instruction, the teacher disappeared in the water and drowned.

******

The important message of the story is that we should take the enlightened approach and not slavishly follow outdated conservative ideas, nor resort to any holy book without using our common sense. On the face of changing circumstances, new discoveries and knowledge, we must learn to adapt ourselves accordingly and respond to them by using them for the benefit of everybody.

Moral Conduct and Youth

It is often said that there is a decline in the standard of morality and discipline amongst the youths today. This certainly does not apply to all youths, but there are many who may be confused and rebellious. Their behaviour and habits violate public peace whereby innocent peace-loving people have to undergo great humiliation and suffering.

In a way, parents are to be blamed for the bad behaviour and lack of consideration on the part of their children. Their permissiveness, encouraged by modern psychologists, have given too much freedom to their children to do as they like. This is often coupled with the fact that parents are themselves too busy looking after their own materialistic needs that they neglect their children. To prevent moral decadence in society, parents have the important duty to nurture and guide their children according to religious and spiritual teachings found in the great world religions.

In the teaching of ethics and morality, religious labels are not important. Every religion has its own moral code designed to regulate human conduct so that people can live together as civilized human beings. Together they can contribute to their communities which offer mutual respect protection, solidarity and moral support. It is very unfortunate, if religionists create discriminations, hostility and jealousy towards the other religious groups.

Being Good or Doing Good?

In his book, Buddhist Ethics, Ven. Dr. H. Saddha-tissa said, 'Generally speaking, there are two ideas of morality: (i) to be good, and (ii) to do good. The first is the real morality, whereas the second may be only a means to an end. One can be good in order to do good, but this is rare. People do good actions which appear entirely altruistic yet fundamentally are egoistic, motivated by acquisitiveness, desire for merit, bliss, heaven, reward or motivated by fear of resulting punishment or hell. All so-called "good" actions are inspired by selfishness and to the Buddhist the idea of "being" good is the only true morality.'

The person who admits the evil deeds committed by him is at least better than the person who tries to justify his evil deeds, and who denies and pretends that he is innocent. Shakespeare expresses this beauti-fully when Lady Macbeth urges her husband before he kills the king to *be like the innocent flower but be the serpent under it.*' A person who is openly evil can at least be avoided, but the hypocrite's evil intentions are not seen until it is too late.

What shall it profit a man, though he be rich, fortunate and enjoying all the rewards of the past good kamma, when he is not virtuous, charitable and bene-volent in this present life? He is like a man who lives on his capital, constantly drawing from his bank account of good kamma but without replenishing it. When it is all exhausted, he will proceed to his future existence as a spiritual pauper. Whom should he blame for his miserable condition – god or fate? Neither: he has only himself to be blamed.

In the human situation, the agony of choosing which action to perform, whether good or bad, is perpetually with us. In such circumstances, we should know the terms under which our choice is to be made. As surely as water seeks its own level, so does kamma. Given the right conditions, kamma will produce its inevitable results which are not to be regarded as reward or punishment, but only as natural course of events. To the weak-willed, the knowledge of the workings of kamma serves as a deterrent towards doing evil, while to the spiritually advanced it encourages him to do good.

The philosopher, Santayana, pointed out that *the greatest difficulty in life lies not so much as making the choice between good and evil as the choice between good and good.* When still young, we do not realise that one desire can be quite inconsistent with another. A young boy may hesitate between a dozen different plans for the future, but a mature man will have to renounce many careers in order to fulfill one duty.

The same applies to emotions. While we can understand the adolescent who transfers his love-interest from one object of affection to another, it is mockery when a grown man still acts like an adolescent. The man who wears the youth's carefree clothing and the woman who costumes her emotions in doll's dresses are pathetic figures. They have yet to learn that human growth requires the closing of many doors before one great door can be opened – the door of mature love and wholesome achievements.

Aristotle said: *'The ideal man takes joy in doing favours for others, but he feels ashamed to have others to do favours for him.'* It is often considered a mark of superiority to confer kindness, but one of inferiority to receive it. In Buddhism, however, the giving and receiving of kindness should be done with equanimity without the feeling of superiority or inferiority, without ulterior motives, and without hopes of material or spiritual reward. In this way, the motivation for the action is utterly pure, untainted by even the slightest sense of selfishness.

Changing One's Character Through Religion

A tree is known by its fruit. Similarly, a true religion must produce permanent results. In this sense, it is quite right to judge a religion by its results.

When a person has embraced a religion, the teachings should help to improve his behaviour. But if he continues to be just as greedy, spiteful, and envious as before, if he cheats those who work for him, or robs his neighbour, if he shows no compassion for suffering fellow beings, or at the slightest provocation he plunges a knife into the bosom of another – then these teachings are ineffective as far as he is concerned.

Mere belief, emotional feeling or glorification of a person's own religion mean nothing unless he improves his behaviour and acts with gentleness. This may be likened to an illness in which a person may be 'feeling better' but is not really so since the thermometer shows that his temperature is still rising.

A religion which enables us to understand better the nature of life can enable us to accept the various forms of happiness as it arises during the various phases of our life. We should be able to welcome them when they come, and to let them go without regret when they are gone. This fact is proclaimed by William Blake when he wrote:

'He who catches the joy as it flies,
Lives in eternity's sunrise.'

The practice of a religion enables one to undergo spiritual transformation which arises from within, rather than from without. It is not external appearance that makes a person noble, but internal purification and an exemplary life. Rank, caste, colour and even wealth and power do not necessarily make a gentleman. Only character makes a person great and worthy of honour.

Your wealth can decorate your house,
but only your virtue can decorate you.
Your dress can decorate your body,
but only your conduct can decorate you.

Morality should not be taken to apply only at a personal level, but to be practised by all members of society. For there to be peace in society, its members must not cut spiritual corners. A person may think that he can get away with the performance of evil deeds. He may even be tempted to adopt the bad moral values glorified on TV. But nobody can escape the consequences of his evil deeds, and no society can be peaceful as long as there are such people around.

In addition, for there to be peace and happiness in a society, people in positions of power should uphold moral principles since their actions have profound effects on those who are below them. The Buddha said:

'When the ruler of a country is just and good, the ministers will become just and good. When the ministers are just and good, the higher officials will become just and good. When the higher officials are just and good, the rank and file will become just and good. When the rank and file are just and good, the people will become just and good.'

16

YOU MAKE YOUR LUCK
AND DESTINY

'The fool may watch for lucky days
Yet luck he shall always miss.
Luck itself is luck's own star
What can mere stars achieve.'

~ *Buddhist Jataka Story* ~

Belief in good luck or bad luck is very common amongst the masses. It is due to lack of understanding of the law of kamma, worldly conditions and the nature of phenomena that people attribute sudden windfall to good luck and downfall to bad luck. The Buddha taught us that good effects, that is to say good results, come from good causes, and bad results from bad causes in accordance with the law of kamma. When a person faces the bad effects of his evil deeds performed during his present or past lives, he should not blame it on his bad luck. Instead it would be more correct for him to say that he is experiencing the effects of his bad kamma. Anyone who understands the law of kamma will not make the mistake of believing in luck because he knows that whatever happens to him is the result of a cause or causes brought about by negative thinking and immoral acts performed by him in the past. This way, he can understand that he is responsible for his own happiness or unhappiness based on how well or how badly he leads his life. There is no such thing as luck. The choice is up to us.

Don't Blame the Stars

Although the Buddha has not denied the influence of certain stars and planets on people, weak-hearted people generally succumb to what they think are the influences of such stars and planets. Their imagination and fear will only tend to aggravate the already tense situation, creating frustration and distress. But all those with strong will-power, courage, intelligence and self-confidence can succeed in their careers and overcome difficulties without being enslaved by such influences. Luck and skilfulness are closely related. It all goes back again to the power of the mind, the potential of which every individual can develop.

Man should not surrender himself and give up his struggle against misfortune on the pretext that he does not have good luck. Nor should he allow himself to fall victim to such beliefs which would only hinder his own material and spiritual progress. Even if his career is a failure due to his bad kamma, he can overcome or at least minimise its bad effects by maintaining a healthy mind and doing more good. He can do good in many ways, in kind or by deed without having to spend money. He can, for instance, perform meritorious deeds by practising tolerance, patience, goodwill and understanding.

According to Buddhism, effort is the most important condition by which one can modify the unfolding of one's bad kamma. By effort made today, a person can create fresh kamma, and change his environment and circumstances. It is always possible for one to change his own kamma. If his failure is due to his own inefficiency, inexperience or laziness, he must try to improve himself and learn how to overcome his failure without blaming the stars, devils or spirits. An understanding of his own nature and an admission of his own weaknesses to himself is the first step towards reforming himself.

Destiny is in Your Hands

There is no such thing as inevitable fate or irrevocable destiny according to the teachings of the Buddha. If we examine our own experiences and those of others, we will realise that the unhappiness and suffering experienced today are the results of faults that had been committed yesterday.

＊＊*＊*

You gave me bad luck. Kalidasa was a famous Sanskrit poet who lived in India during the third century A.D. As a young boy, he was poor and lived with his mother in a small hut facing the king's palace. Within the palace walls was a large orchard of mango trees. During the fruit season, the trees were heavy with sweet, delicious mangoes. When no one was watching, Kalidasa would climb over the walls and help himself to the mangoes.

One day when Kalidasa was stealing the mangoes, he did not realise that the king was watching him from the palace window. That morning, while the king was peeling a mango, he accidentally cut his hand. Since the cut drew a lot of blood, the king summoned his Wise men and fortune tellers to tell him the significance of that accident.

The Wise men thought for a while and asked the king if he saw anything unusual that morning. The king replied that he saw a boy stealing some mangoes from the palace ground. 'Oh! what your majesty saw was very inauspicious. That boy will bring you bad luck,' said the Wise men. 'It is good if your majesty could get rid of him immediately.'

The king ordered that Kalidasa be brought before him. As the poor trembling boy stood before the king, he was told that the king had seen him stealing the mangoes and this had brought the king bad luck. He was asked if he had anything to say before he was taken away for execution.

'I'm very sorry for bringing you bad luck, Your Majesty,' said Kalidasa. 'But it is reasonable to also punish accordingly the person who saw me this morning because as you can see he has brought me bad luck too.' That reply surprised the king as he realised that he was a fool to have listened to the fortune tellers who called themselves Wise men. Being impressed with Kalidasa, the king adopted him as his son. It was in the palace that Kalidasa developed his literary skills and later emerged as a famous poet in India.

＊＊＊＊＊＊

Man is not a mere pawn on a chessboard of universal forces over which he has no control. His destiny is something entirely self-created and self-earned, whether it is for good or for evil. Man creates his own destiny by his own thoughts, words and deeds, and he gets back from life sooner or later what he himself has given to life. From the consequences of his deeds there is no escape. Hence, man himself is the builder of his own life, the creator of his fate, now and in the future.

The law of kamma which shapes the outcome of one's destiny has no sense of retribution. There is no motive of punishment in that great universal force. Nature is impartial. It cannot be flattered nor does it grant special favours upon request. When suitable conditions arise, the deeds which we have planted will bear results. Therefore, in the face of calamities, no good is gained by crying out against the heavens. We must learn to understand the nature of worldly conditions which are marked with uncertainty and bear the seemingly 'unjust' suffering with a calm mind.

The effect of kamma on one's destiny will not be unchanging. Therefore, the concept of eternal suffering or everlasting heavenly bliss is alien to Buddhism. All states of being in the cycle of birth and death (Samsara) are impermanent. Only when one is freed from relative existence in Samsara and has attained Nibbana can eternal bliss be realised.

The process of cultivating spiritual maturity encompasses self-training and moral discipline, mental purification, and leading a righteous way of life, filled with loving-kindness, harmony and selfless service. Various religions give different interpretations of how salvation from suffering is possible. In the case of Buddhism, a person can be liberated by living in accordance with the universal moral laws and by purifying his mind. He can thereby shape his own destiny without becoming over-dependent on forces external to himself.

As human beings, we must not waste our human existence by grieving over the past or passing our time in idleness and heedlessness. This way we will only squander away the opportunity to realise the real purpose of our life and retard our progress towards complete liberation from suffering. We must strongly bear this in mind, and do good while life lasts. By wasting our time, not only will we mislead others, but we also miss the golden opportunity to achieve something in our valuable human life.

'There is nothing like destiny other than the effect of our previous efforts. Our previous efforts are called our destiny......Our achievements are determined by our efforts. Our effort is therefore our destiny....Our previous and present efforts, in case they are in contrary directions, are like two rams fighting against each other. The more powerful of the two always overthrowing the other....Whether they are the past or present efforts, it is the stronger ones that determine our destiny. In either case, it is man's own effort which determines his destiny by virtue of its strength ....Man determines his own destiny by his own thought. He can make those things also happen which were not destined to happen. Only those things happen in this world which he creates through his own free efforts and not others....One should therefore overcome one's unfavourable destiny (the effect of one's past effort) by the greater effort in the present. There is nothing in this world which cannot be achieved by men through the right sorts of effort.'

'Everything has its beauty, but not every one sees it.'

~ Confucius ~

PART IV

TECHNIQUES FOR HAPPY AND SUCCESSFUL LIVING

17

SACRIFICING FOR OTHERS' WELFARE

Great people always regard their body of flesh and blood as useful just for the world's good and welfare.

Different answers can be heard when people are asked which is more important, their money or their lives. To a miser, his money is more important. To a wealthy man, his life is more important. And to a great man, his principles are far more important than his money or life. But such great people are rare and only a handful can be counted. That is why we regard them as great people. Sometimes for adhering to their principles and refusing to surrender under any circumstances, they are persecuted by their fellow-men. Socrates was poisoned, Jesus crucified, and Gandhi assassinated.

Truly great people have one thing in common, that is, they use their resources – wisdom, sympathy, power, energy, knowledge – for the good and benefit of mankind. They understand that it is not possible to do the highest good to themselves without also doing it to others as well. The Buddha said that one should first establish oneself in what is proper, then instruct others. Such a wise person will not become remorseful.

A person may be very intelligent, but if he abuses it for his own selfish desires, then from the Buddhist standpoint he is considered to have neglected himself badly. Such an attitude will bring him no good. Albert Schweitzer, the Nobel Prize winner, said: '*The only ones among you who will be truly happy are those who have sought and found how to serve.*' Ruth Smeltzer writes:

'*Some measure their lives by days and years,*
Others by heart throbs, passion and tears;
But the surest measure under the sun,
Is what in your lifetime for others you have done.'

Many people think that making sacrifices means giving more than they are prepared to give. Actually, this is not the case since everything depends on one's perception of values and the degree of unselfishness one has developed. A person who has personal needs regards them as being secondary when he perceives that the needs of others are more urgent. There is a true story to illustrate this point.

******

Control sorrow by helping others. Once there was a doctor who founded a free clinic which opened once a week to attend to poor patients. On one such day, someone rushed in to the clinic with the news that the doctor's youngest and favourite son had just died. Although deeply upset, the doctor reflected on the situation, and after having regained his composure, continued to attend to his patients.

People who came to know about this, were rather surprised at his seemingly callous behaviour. When questioned, he explained thus: 'My son is already dead and I am unable to assist him any more. But these poor needy patients who can't even afford to pay for their treatment need my help more. I know I can do something for them. So is it not better for me to control my sorrow and help suffering mankind instead?'

******

Doing good to others is not a duty. It is a privilege, and it gives pleasure leading to better health and happiness.

~ *Zoroaster* ~

Kindness to All Beings

Often people have thoughtlessly, and sometimes even

deliberately, aggravated the discomfort and suffering of others. It is the uncultured mentality in man that takes delight in the pain and agony of others. If they themselves do not like to be hurt, what right have they to inflict pain on others? The Buddha says, *'He who loves himself should injure none.'*

Treat others as you would like to be treated. This golden rule is endorsed by all religious teachers. Yet, people have often disregarded the fact that life is dear to every living being, and as testimony to this callousness in human behaviour we can turn to the history of mankind which is filled with massacres, bloodshed and torture. We have seen that for some, killing has even become a hobby or a pastime. Such sub-human behaviour has soaked man's past with blood. For this reason, some people have regarded the History of Mankind as the History of Insanity and Inhumanity.

'We should not do unto others what we do not wish done unto ourselves.' This is an old saying but it is still relevant today. In the same breath we also add: *'We should do unto others as we wish others do unto us.'* These sayings should be practised to overcome the generally selfish and self-centered nature of men who are only interested in themselves and have no time for others.

✵✵✵✵✵✵

Concentrate more on your duty. There are some do-gooders in this world who busy themselves with other people's affairs and then get themselves into trouble in the process. Have you heard of the story of the donkey which tried to do the dog's job? Well, once there was a man who owned a dog and a donkey. One night the dog kept his master awake with its constant howling and the master was so annoyed that he beat up the dog. Now the dog was in so much pain that it spent the whole of the following day and night sulking in a corner. As luck would have it, that very night some thieves entered the house, but the dog disregarded its duty and kept silent. The donkey was outside, watching all that was going on. He said to himself, 'Look, my master is asleep, the thieves are robbing him and the dog is not doing its duty. I must take over the dog's duties immediately and begin to bray as loudly as I can.' The donkey did this with a good intention though it was not its duty. The master woke up from his sleep, and shouted, 'What is this? Last night it was the dog, now it is this stupid donkey.' So saying he got out of his bed, in a rage, grabbed the whip and lashed the donkey, causing it severe pain. The donkey soon realised its lesson and lamented, 'Ah! those who try to perform the duties of others without being told to do so will surely get themselves a good whipping.'

****

The Spirit of Benevolence

Life is precious to all living beings. All beings shrink

with fear at the mere thought of being deprived of their lives. As we do not wish for death, other beings also do not wish for it. As we are frightened at the mere thought of death, so are other beings. Therefore, we should not kill nor cause to kill any living being, however small or insignificant. We must open up the storehouse of virtue within us to feel for those who are less fortunate than ourselves and try to help them.

Buddhism teaches us not to hurt or kill any being intentionally. It encourages us to love and protect all beings. If everyone in our society can learn to be benevolent and grateful, or be ready to reciprocate, even in a small way, the kindness shown to each person, then human society will become more peaceful and pleasant to live with. Human relationship, like the law of action and reaction, is a two-way traffic. When love and mutual respect is practised in private as well as in public life, clashes or misunderstandings that upset goodwill and good relationships will be eliminated.

We should always strive to help and serve others. At the same time, we should not neglect the training and development of our understanding so that we can see things as they are and not what they appear to be. This we will be able to do by using our common sense. When we are going to help others, it is very important for us to know who or what they are and their attitude, in order that we can be mindful to handle them with care.

Beware of whom you help. Innocent people may

help the wicked but they should do so wisely otherwise they also face problems and get into trouble.
Although every religion appreciates such services, it
must be done with understanding.

****

Beware of wicked ones. A man once saw a tiger caught
in a net. The tiger pleaded with the man to set him free
but the man said, 'No, you will eat me if I set you
free.' But the tiger begged, pleaded and promised the
man that not only would he leave him alone, he would
even be his protector for life. The foolish man believed
the tiger and removed the net. Needless to say, the
ungrateful tiger pounced on him. The man screamed
in fright and this attracted the attention of a fox who
came to see what the commotion was all about. The
man told the fox how he released the tiger. The tiger
however claimed that the man did not do very much
to release him. While they were thus arguing, the fox
said, 'Hey wait. I am all confused. If you want me to
settle this matter, I must know how it all began. Now,
I want to see where the tiger was when you came.'
The man began to explain but the fox said, 'I still
don't understand. Show me how the tiger was
caught.' The foolish tiger entered the net again. When
he was sure the beast was properly trapped, the fox
turned to the man and said, 'Now go your way and
beware of wicked ones who make promises they never
intend to keep.'

****

The Real Conqueror

Today, people are trying to dominate each other. People often strive hard for money, power and position so that they will have control over others. It will be to one's benefit if we could only realise that it is more important to first conquer oneself. The Buddha said that self conquest is better than world conquest, and renunciation of worldly pleasures is better than accumulation of all the riches of the world. Everyone should make every effort to conquer one's anger, jealousy, pride, greed and other shortcomings. Courage, determination and perseverance are needed to control and overcome these destructive forces.

A few weeks before Mahatma Gandhi died at the hands of an assassin's bullet, he had a visitor who wondered how Mahatmaji could marshal so much courage though of frail body and Gandhi had said that courage is not part of the physique but of the mind.

Though one should conquer a thousand times a thousand men in battle, he who conquers his own self is the greatest of all conquerors.

~ Gautama Buddha ~

If we can conquer ourselves, others will trust and respect us for our victory. The Buddha conquered himself first and then he conquered the whole world with his love, compassion and wisdom. Thus, he is widely respected by Buddhists and non-Buddhists alike. Man must understand that he is the master of his own destiny. His happiness and sadness are entirely of his own making. Therefore, by understanding this, we must adjust ourselves accordingly to lead respectable and peaceful lives. To do this, we must seek the necessary guidance and instructions in a rational religion which can give us the liberty to think freely and which does not resort to any form of blind faith.

Man must understand that the results he reaps are in accordance with his deeds. If he wallows in destructive emotions, he will place himself in constant danger. When bad thoughts arise in his mind, he must act wisely by controlling his mind. Through the cultivation of his mind, he will spontaneously find happiness and purpose in wholesome deeds, speech and thoughts. In the book Buddhist Meditation, Venerable Dr. Vajiranana wrote: *'If meditation or mental cultivation is successful, positive expression of Metta (loving-kindness) will be the driving force for our actions. That is to say, the mental attitudes of benevolence and goodwill, when it is expanding in the heart, must find outward expression in real acts of kindness.'*

Man is living in a world influenced by many forces. It is important for him to understand the nature of worldly conditions so as to know how to adjust his way of life, either to face them or to overcome them. He will then know where his place in human society is, and how to live in harmony with the universal law and other living beings. If the world is chaotic, it is only because man has made it so. Conversely, it is within the power of man to change the quality of the whole atmosphere by generating benevolent thoughts and actions with skill. By so doing, man will not only work towards his own spiritual growth, but also share in shaping the destiny of the whole world for the benefit of all beings.

Human Values

The rules to develop human values in Buddhism are simple. One must work hard and be conscientious. One must not waste one's time unnecessarily, idling away and doing nothing. Even regarding sleep, one must be rational by keeping it to the minimum necessary for health. One should not give lame excuses that either the day is too hot or too cold for the allotted work to be done. Be constructive and conscientious in whatever you do. It was recorded that the Buddha Himself was the most energetic and active religious teacher who has ever lived in this world. During His forty five years of noble service to mankind, it was reputed that He only slept for a period of two hours each day. He travelled all over the country advising people how to lead a noble way of life.

'A long life may be not good enough, but a good life is long enough'

~ Benjamin Franklin ~

18

GENTLE SPEECH

'Much talking is a source of danger,
Through silence misfortune is avoided,
The talkative parrot in a cage is shut,
While birds that cannot talk fly freely.'

~ *Tibetan Yogi* ~

Once four intimate friends promised one another to observe seven days of silence in quiet meditation. On the first day all were silent, and the meditation went on as scheduled. But when night came, the oil-lamp they were using ran out of oil and started to flicker. A servant was dozing off nearby. One of them could not help but say to the servant: 'Fix the lamp'.

The second friend was horrified to hear the first one speaking. 'Hush,' he said, 'We are not supposed to say a word, remember?'

'Both of you are stupid. Why did you talk?' said the third. Very softly, the fourth muttered, 'I was the only one who didn't say anything.'

******

Man has been able to rise above animals and build great civilizations and complex social systems because of his ability to communicate through speech and writing. Not only is he able to communicate with contemporaries, he is also able to set his ideas in writing to communicate with future generations long after he is dead.

In modern society, communications play a crucial role in human relationships. From birth, we have the inborn urge to talk and communicate with those we come into contact with. Well used, words can help us a great deal. But often, we speak hastily without thinking about what we are going to say. Like the four friends in the story mentioned earlier, quite often we wish we had not said something after it had been uttered. By then, it is too late since words once spoken can never be withdrawn. We may apologise and retract them, but the damage is already done.

Another writer says, 'Words are the dress of thoughts which should no more be presented in rags, tatters and dirt than your person should.'

Wrong Speech

It is apparent that amongst all living beings, humans are known as the biggest liars. You must have witnessed the trouble and commotion caused by wrong speech, such as lies, unjust speech, caustic remarks, gossip, and unfounded rumours.

Some people can escape and survive anywhere after cheating others because of their tactful and cunning way of talking while innocent people get into trouble. So people must associate with them wisely.

******

What happened to the brain? There is an old story about a lion who longed to eat his favourite delicacy, buffalo meat. There was in the forest just such a buffalo, but try as he might, he was unable to catch this tasty beast. So he decided to use his cunning to get what he wanted. He called his assistant, a fox, and said to him, 'You know, I really don't understand why we live in fear of each other. Please go and tell the buffalo that from now on I have decided to become a vegetarian and invite him to share my den with him.' The fox went to the buffalo and conveyed the message. The buffalo was suspicious at first, but the fox argued that the lion was really harmless. After all had he himself not lived with this lion for a long time? Finally the buffalo was convinced. He came into the cave, was courteously treated and thus assured, he lay down to sleep. The lion wasted no more time. Upon a flash he pounced on the poor buffalo and killed him with one stroke. Now the lion's favourite was buffalo brain and though he was very hungry, all the waiting had tired him. So he decided to take a rest and instructed the fox to guard the carcass while he slept. Of course, now the fox also craved buffalo brain, and so while his master slept, he opened up the skull, and ate the delicious brain. Thus satisfied he cleverly replaced the skull and, with an innocent look on his face waited for his master to awake. The lion woke up and eagerly went to enjoy his delicacy but great was his surprise and anger when he opened the head and found it empty. Furiously he demanded an explanation from the fox who replied: 'Master, the reason the skull is empty is that this buffalo had no brain. Do you think if it had any brain it could have fallen for your trick?'

******

The Buddha spoke about the four kinds of wrong speech. The first is lying. When a person goes to a court of justice, or is in the company of relatives and friends, he would say 'I know' when he does not, and 'I don't know' when he does. To save himself, or for the sake of some small gain, he deliberately utters lies.

The second is backbiting. When a person wanders here or there, he spreads falsehood around to cause disruption. He breaks up fellowship, does not reconcile those at strife, finds pleasure and delight in quarrels, and utters words to incite others to quarrel.

The third is harsh speech. The words spoken are insolent and rude, bitter for others to hear. People always accuse others, even for minor mistakes yet keep quiet when the latter do some good deeds. One writer says: *'When I am good everybody forgets, but when I am bad everybody remembers.'*

The fourth is idle babbling. This speech is made by a person speaking out of turn on things non-existent or irrelevant. His speech is unrestrained, out of place, thoughtless and does not bring any benefit whatsoever.

The next time before we speak, we must think before opening our mouths. The injunction 'Think before you speak' can help us avoid getting into disputes or arguments and avoid hurting others unnecessarily. We must analyse our thoughts and intentions before expressing them. We must not only know what to say, but also why, when, where and how to say it.

A wise man knows how to avoid problems by being careful about what he says. There is a saying that even a fish will not get caught on a hook if he knows how to keep his big mouth shut at the right time. There is a fable to illustrate this truth.

✳✳✳✳✳✳

The fox who had a cold. Once there was an old lion who was very hungry but he was too weak to go out hunting. However he had an attendant, a fox, who had served him for many years. Now the lion was desperately hungry and decided that the only thing he could do was eat the fox. But, being the king of the beasts he could not very well just pounce on the fox, so he decided to find an excuse to kill his faithful attendant. He called the fox to him and said, 'Fox, I am going to ask you a question which you must answer truthfully. If you don't give the right answer I will kill you. Tell me, am I pleasant smelling or foul smelling?' Fox clearly saw the trap. If he said the lion was foul smelling the lion would be insulted and kill him. If he said the lion was pleasant smelling, he would be called a liar and would get killed anyway. So the fox thought carefully and replied, 'Master, I am afraid you asked that question at a wrong time. You see, I am suffering from a very bad cold and my nose is blocked, so I really cannot tell how you smell. In fact I am worried that I will pass my cold on to you. So out of concern for your health I am going to leave you and go far away from you.'

The wise man knows how to get himself out of a tricky situation by saying the right thing at the right time.

******

Angry words can be followed by blows. A person in control of the situation will not be easily provoked into a fight or to act unwisely. Always remember that your battle is lost, the moment you lose your balance. Indeed, it is very rewarding to observe and see the effect you can generate on others by refusing to allow yourself to be provoked. They would get more and more irritated because they cannot make you angry, and they will realise that you are the winner. Take the opportunity to study human nature. How silly people look when they lose their temper. Similarly you should also realise how silly you look when you lose your temper.

Acting Wisely in Tense Situations

We can avoid heated arguments by acting wisely. Sometimes a situation becomes tense because of certain things said or done which upset people. Some people take strong positions in a discussion by raising their voices which soon leads to the quickening of everyone's heart beat. Under such circumstances, we should use some tact to try to diffuse the explosive situation.

******

If I am not mad, how can I say you are mad? There was a temperamental old man. His moods changed so quickly that he would joke and laugh at one moment and then explode in anger at another moment. This happened very often when he visited his friend's house so much so that many people were disturbed by his behaviour. One day, his friend remarked that maybe there was something wrong with his mind.

When he heard what was said about him, the old man became very angry. He confronted his friend and demanded. 'Why did you say I'm mad?' He looked dead serious and was ready to start a quarrel.

The friend realised that he should not have made the remark, but what could he do now? Since he was a religious man he did not like to have a heated argument. Very quickly the friend answered, 'Well, do you know that I'm also mad!'

Surprised, the old man asked, 'How can you say you're mad?'

'Well, my dear friend, if I'm not mad, how can I say you're mad?' On hearing this clever and diplomatic reply, the old man burst into laughter and a potentially big problem was thus solved.

******

It is difficult to discover the truth of a matter through arguments. A person who possesses oratorical skills can turn, twist and hide the facts for his own benefit and easily destroy an opponent's point of view by talking his way out, but he may not come any closer to the truth. Heated arguments never bring any good results. The truth will never emerge from heated arguments, or by hurting the feelings of others with unkind remarks. People who get involved in heated arguments usually become defensive and will find it harder to realise their own mistakes and forget the original issue in question.

On the other hand when some cunning people realise that they cannot either defend or hide their own mistakes, they will normally try to accuse their opponents by bringing forward certain personal weaknesses or some other allegations in order to divert their attention so that their opponents will forget the original charges made against them.

If we wish to know the real facts, we must think quietly and discuss our ideas with others calmly and gently. When we speak slowly, we are in control of our emotions. When we are provoked or our emotions are aroused, we must be mindful so as not to allow ourselves to be carried away by such emotions and act foolishly and blindly. We must not be dictated to by our anger or resentment, to commit unwholesome acts as a result of that provocation. We must be in absolute control of the situation and not allow the situation take control over us. This is the hallmark of a person in control of himself. Silent sense is better than fluent folly.

It is very unfortunate that certain uncultured or narrow minded people, whenever faced with any misunderstanding or argument usually insult the other parties by calling them names and bringing forward their personal matters such as race, caste and colour in disparaging terms. This unpleasant and unhealthy attitude can create enmity or hatred which prevails throughout life and such animosity usually results in violence and bloodshed.

Be Mindful of Thoughts

Those who know the nature of mental activities say

that once a thought is made, whether good or bad, it is permanently implanted within the mind. It is good to ponder on this concept and consider which ideas we should entertain because of the effects such thoughts have on us.

> *The thought manifests as the word,*
> *The word manifests as the deed,*
> *The deed develops into habit,*
> *And the habit hardens into character.*
> *So watch the thought and its way with care,*
> *And let it spring from love*
> *Born out of concern for all beings.*

The words above echo what the Buddha said more than 2500 years ago: 'We are what we think. All that we are arises with our thoughts. With our thoughts we make the world.' The truth of this verse is timeless: it is truth whether for the past, the present or the future.

We should cultivate the habit of being constantly mindful of what we say. Then, we will be able to distinguish between those manners of speech that can annoy people and those that can make them happy. Through this awareness, we will be able to consider the value or otherwise of all our thoughts, words and actions. Thoughts controlled means words controlled.

Words controlled mean actions controlled. When all the senses are controlled persons become harmless and noble.

Cultivating Skilful Speech

It is important to regard our tongue as the servant. We are the master; the tongue will do our bidding. The tongue will have to say what we want to say and not what it wants us to say. Unfortunately, for most of us, it is our tongue that is the master and we are its slave. We have to listen to what it speaks in our name and we seem unable to stop its wagging. The result of such lack of control is always disastrous.

Some people vow to observe silence after a bad experience of wrong speech. They guard their tongue so that no evil word will escape from their lips. But if we live in society, can we maintain silence all the time?

******

We cannot avoid problems either by talking or keeping silent. Once there was a monk who had a lazy attendant boy who would sleep late into the morning. One day he woke the boy up and shouted at him saying, 'You still sleeping! Even the tortoises are out of the pond, lying out in the sun.'

At the time, a man who was trying to catch some tortoises to make a medicinal soup for his mother overheard what the monk had just said and he went to the pond. True enough, there were many tortoises lying out in the morning sun. He caught a few of them and made the soup for his mother. But he had not forgotten about the monk. In gratitude for the monk's advice, he offered him some tortoise soup. The monk was horrified to know that his speech was responsible for the death of those creatures and vowed not to speak again.

Sometime later, the monk was sitting out in the verandah of the temple. He saw a blind man walking down the road and was heading towards the pond. He wanted to ask the blind man to stop walking but then remembered to observe his vow of silence. While he was debating in his mind as to what to do, the blind man meanwhile had walked straight into the pond and was drenched wet. This made the monk feel very bad and he realized that one cannot live in this world simply by keeping silent or by talking. We must use our common sense to survive in this world.

******

There is an art of speaking, and that is, to speak gently and politely, not harshly or rudely. We must learn to speak at the right time and at the right place on any subject if we wish to avoid conflict or criticism.

Tell the truth, nothing but truth. But be wise, if the truth that you are going to tell is unpleasant.

19

THE VALUE OF LOVING KINDNESS

We may not be saintly enough to love our enemies, but for the sake of our health and happiness, let us at least forgive and forget them.

~ Dale Carnegie ~

An ogress was in hot pursuit of a nobleman's daughter and her baby. When the lady heard that the Buddha was teaching Dhamma at the monastery, she visited Him and placed her son at His feet for protection. The ogress was thus prevented from entering the monastery. She was later called in, and both the lady and ogress were admonished by the Buddha.

The Buddha said that in one of their past lives, one of them was barren and that her husband had arranged to marry the other woman. Later when the first wife knew that the other was pregnant, she mixed a drug to the food and thus caused her to have a miscarriage. Two similar attempts were made, and on the third attempt the fruitful wife died. However, before her death, this unfortunate woman, who was in a rage, vowed vengeance on the barren woman and her future offspring.

Thus their past feud as rival wives and the hatred they harboured towards each other led to the killing of each other's children in their various subsequent lives. The ogress' desire to kill the woman's baby was only a continuation of this deep-seated hatred. Hatred can only cause more hatred: it can only cease through love, friendship, understanding and goodwill. Both realised their mistakes, and on the advice of the Buddha, they made peace with each other.

This story tells us how people carry their hatred even after death into their future lives.

****

Loving and Kindness

The pursuit of happiness is not difficult if we have the right mental attitude. Love is the key to happiness. All human beings have the potential to give and receive love. We are potentially storehouses of love.

Love is a priceless gift to bestow on to another.

Through love, we can provide the warmth to satisfy the burning needs of an individual to be loved, for those who love and are loved in return are happier than those devoid of love. The more love we give the more will we receive in return. This is in accordance with the eternal law of cause and effect.

In the Buddha's teachings, the spirit of love is more important than good work. '*All good works whatever are not worth an iota of love which sets free the heart. Love which sets free the heart comprises good work. It shines, gives light and radiance.*'

Love is one of the greatest instruments of nature. The powerful force of love is the bond and cement of society – the spirit and life of the universe. Love is the most precious thing in the world. No matter how unhappy you are now or have been in the past, you can still find happiness in the future. The key to happiness is love, and you are in possession of that precious key, right now and always. And remember, love begins with you. Start the process of extending your love and compassion to all beings. The inevitable reaction will surely be that you will receive plenty of love in return. Telling another person 'I love you' can be a risky business sometimes, but the rewards can be substantial.

Cultivating Loving Kindness

The idea of love can mean different things to various people. Love, according to the Buddha, does not mean attachment to a person or an object through which one desires to satisfy his or her selfish craving. Love should be an endless self-immolating compassion, freely flowing towards all living beings. In the Metta Sutta, the Buddha said:

Let not one deceive another
Nor despise any person whatsoever in any place.
In anger or ill-will,
Let him not wish any harm to another.

Just as a mother would protect her only child,
At the risk of her own life,
Even so let him cultivate a boundless heart
Towards all beings.

Love is the soil in which the loved ones grow. It enriches the other person without limiting or restricting him. Love elevates humanity. Love costs nothing. Love should not be selective. Some may think of love as something to receive, but it is basically a giving process.

In cultivating love and kindness, we should start with those at home. The love between father and mother greatly influences the atmosphere at home and generates love, care and sharing among other family members. A husband and wife should treat each other with respect, courtesy and fidelity.

Parents should fulfil five duties for their children: avoid doing evil and set an example of good deeds, give them an education, be supportive and understanding in their children's love affairs or arrange for their marriage, and let them inherit the family wealth at a proper time. A child, on the other hand, should honour his parents and do for them all he is supposed to do. He should serve them, help them at their labour, cherish the family lineage, protect the family property, do some services to others in their name and hold memorial services for them after they have passed away. If husbands and wives, as well as parents and children follow this advice taught by the Buddha, there will always be happiness and peace in the home. Life is made up of little things in which smiles and kindness and small obligations, given habitually, are what win and preserve the heart.

One mark of a loving person is that he has a compassionate heart. We should cultivate the habit of helping those in trouble and who are less fortunate than ourselves. One should not merely be sympathetic to another emotionally, but should seek to translate that feeling into positive actions. Extending love and kindness does not mean showering gifts, but the showering of gentleness and generosity of spirit. *Kindness is a virtue that the blind can see and the deaf can hear.* So long as there is one single person whom you can console by words, whom you can enliven and cheer by your presence, whom you can relieve by your help, however insignificant or unimportant it might be, you are a precious possession to the human race and you should never be disheartened or depressed. *'Almost anything good you do will seem insignificant,'* says Gandhi, *'but it is very important that you do it.'*

Search for someone less fortunate or less healthy than yourself. Extend any possible help or assistance you can within your means and ability. Make sympathy, empathy and loving kindness keep pace with your capacity for self development. You can be cheated or let down by another and there is none in this world who has not faced such crafty individuals. *There is no shame or humiliation if you are cheated, but it is a shame if you do so to others.* Never harbour thoughts of revenge against those who have wronged you.

There may be times when those you love do not seem to care, and you are apt to feel heavy at heart. But there is no just cause for dejection. What does it matter if others are not grateful to you or do not care for you, as long as you believe that you are full of compassion and love for others.

> 'There is brightness all around,
> When there's love at home,
> There is joy in every sound,
> When there's love at home,
> Time will softly, sweetly glide,
> When there's love at home.'

Gratitude is a rare virtue today. For our own happiness, we should not expect to be appreciated for every act we do. If we expect that, we are bound to face disappointments and frustrations. If honours or recognition come our way, so be it: if not, never mind.

20

TOLERANCE, PATIENCE AND CONTENTMENT

'To live in the world and be intolerant of another's race, religion, customs and colour is like being born an eskimo and having an aversion to snow.'

Tolerance is an important virtue in the Buddhist moral code. We should cultivate tolerance because it helps us to avoid problems. It also helps us to understand other people's troubles, to avoid giving destructive criticism, and to realise that even the finest human being is not infallible. We will also realise that some of the weaknesses found in our neighbours can be found in our own selves as well.

A spiritually enlightened person is likely to be more

tolerant than others. A tolerant person does not like to interfere with another person's freedom of thought, which is the birthright of every individual. He is not easily offended and grants the possibility that others could also be right even if he does not agree with their views. He is not stubborn or unreasonable with his views. If he thinks the other person is wrong, he may try to persuade him to see the error of his by clear reasoning, but never will he force another to accept his views.

One of the greatest tragedies in human relationships is the inability and unwillingness to tolerate and accommodate views that are different. If, on account of religious views, people of different faiths cannot meet on a common platform like cultured people, then surely the missions of the compassionate religious teachers have failed miserably. At such platforms, it would be better to discuss and exchange those views which we agree on and tolerate those which we do not. When certain disturbances arise we must know how to overcome them without aggravating the situation.

******

How to avoid disturbances. There was a headman in a certain village who had a hot tempered father. Each time the elderly man lost his temper, he would storm out of his house and scold his son. Although his temper was well known in the village, this outburst caused some embarrassment and often disturbed others' minds.

One day, the headman hung an iron ring outside his house and instructed the village boys to strike it repeatedly each time his father scolded him. The loud clanging noise drew a lot of attention, and soon the elderly man realised that he was making a fool of himself and stopped scolding his son.

******

Patience

In our daily life, there is much that we have to endure. We have to bear all kinds of pain, both physically and mentally. We have to face worries, frustrations, depressions, and all types of imaginary fears. It is useful to know how to put up with this pain because many physical disorders are brought about by wrong habits of thought, unhealthy mental attitudes and unnecessary anxieties. Under such circumstances, it will be useful to practise patience.

Patience is mentioned as one of the exemplary characteristics of a religious man, along with sincerity, swiftness in understanding and tenderness. One who has these four qualities is said to be worthy of respect.

******

Follow the Buddha's examples. On one occasion the Buddha was invited by a brahmin for alms to his house. As invited, the Buddha visited the house of the brahmin. Instead of entertaining Him, the brahmin poured forth a torrent of abuse with the filthiest of words.

The Buddha politely inquired:–

' Do visitors come to your house, good brahmin? '

' Yes ', He replied.

' What do you do when they come? '

'Oh, we prepare a sumptuous feast.'

'If they fail to turn up?'

' Why, we gladly partake of it. '

' Well, good brahmin, you have invited me for alms and entertained me with abuse which I decline to accept. Please take it back. '

The Buddha did not retaliate, but politely gave back what the Brahmin had given Him. Retaliate not, the Buddha advised. 'Hatreds do not cease through hatred, but through love alone they cease. '

There was no religious teacher highly praised and so severely criticised, reviled and blamed like the Buddha. Such is the fate of great men.

In a public assembly a vile woman named Cinca, pretending to be pregnant, accused the Buddha. With a smiling face the Buddha patiently endured the insult and thereby His innocence was proved.

The Buddha was once accused of murdering a woman assisted by His disciples. Non-Buddhists severely criticised the Buddha and His disciples to such an extent that the Venerable Ananda appealed to the Buddha to leave for another village.

'How, Ananda, what if those other villagers also abuse us?'

'Well then, Lord we will proceed to another village.'

'Then Ananda, the whole of India will have no place for us. Be patient.

These unfounded abuses will automatically cease.

Magandiya, a lady of harem who hated the Buddha for speaking about the repulsiveness of her attractive figure when her father, through ignorance, wished to give her in marriage to the Buddha. She hired drunkards to insult the Buddha in public. With perfect equanimity the Buddha endured the insult. But Magandiya had to suffer for her misdeed.

Insults are a common lot which humanity has to face and endure. The more we work and the greater we become, the more we would be subject to insults and humiliation.

******

The Power of Patience

After gaining spiritual liberation, Pindola, a disciple of the Buddha, returned to his native place, Kosambi, to repay the people there for the kindness they had shown him. It had been a hot summer day, and on reaching the outskirts of Kosambi, Pindola sat in meditation under the cool shade of a tree in a park on the bank of the Ganges River.

At that time, King Udena came to the park with his

consorts for recreation and, after music and pleasure, he took a nap in the shade of another tree. While their King was asleep, his wives and ladies-in-waiting took a walk and suddenly came upon Pindola in meditation. They recognised him as a holy man and asked him to teach them.

When the King awoke from his nap, he went in search of his ladies and found them surrounding this holy man and listening to his teaching. Being of a jealous and lascivious mind, the King became angry and abused Pindola, saying: 'It is inexcusable that you, a holy man, should be in the midst of women and enjoy idle talk with them.' Pindola quietly closed his eyes and remained silent.

The angry King drew his sword and threatened Pindola, but the holy man remained silent and was firm as a rock. This made the King more angry and he broke open an anthill and threw some of the ant-filled dirt upon him. Still Pindola remained sitting in meditation and quietly endured the insult and pain.

Thereupon, the King became ashamed of his bad conduct and begged Pindola's pardon. As a result of this incident, the Buddha's teaching found its way into the King's castle and from there it spread all over the country.

Be patient. Anger leads on to a pathless jungle. While anger irritates and annoys others, it also hurts oneself, weakens the physical frame and disturbs the mind. A harsh word, like an arrow discharged from a bow, can never be taken back even after a thousand apologies. Never use harsh words in a heated argument. It is always the retort that starts the trouble.

By cultivating and developing patience, the destructive emotional energy within us will not have the chance to surface to take control and direct us to commit evil.

******

I did not hear what you said. Once Venerable Sariputta, the chief disciple of the Buddha, was confronted by a brahmin who abused him with angry words. When these words did not affect Venerable Sariputta, the brahmin became even more furious.

'Didn't you hear what I have just said?' shouted the angry brahmin. 'Do you have nothing to say to all my insults?'

Venerable Sariputta, smiled gently at the brahmin, and replied, 'Well, my friend, I do hear you loud and clear. But since I know that you have nothing useful to say, I hear only sound vibrations.'

******

Forget every evil or insult; remember every kindness. The world has witnessed enough hatred already. Let the future be based on the broad foundation of loving-kindness, compassion and wisdom. The Buddhist way of dealing with problems is not prescriptive but therapeutic. Hatred or anger, like any other destructive emotion, is to be eradicated not by suppression but by gradually removing its roots.

If we return violence for violence, there can be no end to it. Enmity will give rise to enmity. A desire for revenge will arouse more vengeful thoughts. Resentment can never be conquered by resentment, and hatred only begets hatred. The best approach to these evils is to appease them with the antidotes of sympathy, forgiveness, tolerance and patience. Gandhi says: '*Take an eye for an eye, and the whole world will be blind.*'

21

BEING FRUSTRATED IN LOVE

One should not lower one's dignity or be a nuisance to the other party.

In this world, it is impossible for all our desires to be satisfied. No matter how powerful or influential a person is, he will still experience frustration. The things he doesn't have, he will long for them. When he already has certain things, he longs for some more or for a change. Unfulfilled desire is common to everyone.

In the matters of the heart, the longing for the love of another always brings frustration. When a person falls in love and finds that his or her feelings are not reciprocated, he or she becomes frustrated. This often occurs among young people. Even conditions which are clearly favourable can change unexpectedly. To illustrate:

******

Who married the girl? Once a young man had fallen deeply in love with a girl from another town. He wrote long letters to her daily expressing his love for her. After sending no less than a few hundred letters, he discovered to his horror that she had fallen in love and married the postman who had delivered the letters.

******

Some people fall in love at first sight and remain happy for the rest of their lives. Some others fall in love at first sight, only to realise that it was infatuation and regret it later. But for the most part, love takes time to grow. Therefore, if love does not blossom immediately, a person should not be disheartened too easily. There is a saying that a faint heart never won a fair lady. This is to say that a person who gives up too easily will not be able to marry the one he desires.

Some can conduct themselves maturely and slowly draw the other's attention to their kindness, consideration, steadfastness, and love for the other. One must not be unreasonable or selfish in the expression of one's feelings. After all, human emotions, like all things in nature, are subject to change. When one conducts oneself well, there is every chance that the other will begin to realise the good qualities and develop warm feelings towards the other and all these may take time.

But there must be a limit in trying to win the heart of another, especially when the answer is a clear 'NO' and the person must not go to extremes in expressing the love. One must give the other the right to make one's own decision and respect that decision. There is no law that one's love for another must be reciprocated. In situations when a person's love is not reciprocated, it is best for either party to wish all the happiness for the future well-being and part as friends without causing any hindrances to their own personality or make a nuisance of themselves.

******

Very effective charm. Once a young man wanted the girl of his dreams to return his love for her. He tried by sending her flowers and gifts but the girl did not respond. Having tried various methods but failing to win the girl's love, he finally thought of a plan – a love charm, and he went to a temple to persuade the monk to prepare that charm for him.

'Sorry, we don't make love charms here,' said the monk. 'If the girl has no interest in you, try to find someone else.' But the young man was insistent that he wished her love only.

Unable to persuade him with advice, the monk

tried another method. 'Alright,' said the monk, 'take this oil with you. When you see her the first thing in the morning, apply this oil on her forehead.'

The young man woke up early the following morning and eagerly waited for the girl to emerge from her house. As she came out with a broom in hand to sweep the compound, he ran forward, dipped his finger in the bottle of oil and applied it to her forehead as instructed by the monk.

The girl not only had a nasty fright but became so furious, that she chased him out, beating him with the broom. The young man learned his bitter lesson about love charms, and decided to turn his love to another girl who liked him. In fact, because of this incident, he was wise enough to marry the girl who really loved him.

Breaking Up

In any love relationship, there is always the possibility of breaking up. A relationship which was like a dream had turned sour and the parties involved could see the split coming. In the breakup of a relationship there is pain, especially when one's emotions are all tied up in knots. Emotional knots have to be cut sooner or later, and each time they are cut the parties involved bleed a little. One should accept the fact that for some time, one will be subjected to sharp fluctuations in emotions. Memories of things said or done could suddenly arise and fill one with a flood of emotions.

In such a situation, some people walk around like a wounded victim. If there is nothing that one can do about the breakup, the very first thing is to *accept its inevitability*. Until one does that, one can be paralyzed, with thoughts running over and over in the mind of how to mend something that cannot be mended. One must be prepared to undergo a few stages emotionally before recovering from the breakup.

At first, there will be the *shock*. One will find it hard to believe that the breakup has really happened. After the shock will be one's *injured sense of pride*. One has lost face, especially to oneself. After the shock and finding a way to salvage the pride, one has to face the *loneliness* of being alone. But even this will go away eventually. It is not going to go away in a day or a week; it will take time, but *it will go away*. During this period, one should *try living one day at a time*. Don't think about the past or worry too much about the future. Living one day at a time will help one in tiding over the worst days. And then, before one knows it, one is no longer affected by the breakup, and one is really free again.

One should avoid doing something foolish during the period of adjustment. Every now and then, we read in the newspapers about tragedies of suicides, violence and murder committed by the broken-hearted. There was a case of a young man who threw himself into the river and drowned, with his love letters neatly wrapped in a plastic package stuffed in his pocket. He was broken-hearted because his girlfriend had decided to marry another man. This young man had committed physical suicide. Some commit emotional suicide by going insane out of frustration and disappointment due to a broken love affair. Some refuse to marry or to fall in love again after being jilted.

Why do people have to undergo all this suffering? It is because they have not developed an understanding of the uncertainties of life and is, therefore, caught up in an emotional turbulence. They develop attachment and have unreasonable expectations. A person who has a better understanding of the nature of life will know that life is affected by eight wordly conditions. Like the waves in the ocean, these eight worldly conditions fluctuate. One moment it is favourable and is welcomed with open arms; at another moment it becomes unfavourable, which is rather hard to bear. Like a pendulum swinging back and forth, desirable and undesirable conditions prevail in this world and everyone, without exception, must face them.

One may enjoy some gain, but for every gain there is also the danger of loss. This is true for fame, praise and happiness, which have the risk of their negative counterparts, namely, defame, blame and pain, arising. However, the occurrence of every negative condition carries also the hope that things will change for the better. A loss can set the foundation for future gain, while defame can turn into fame, blame into praise, and pain into happiness. Such is the instability of worldly conditions. And the affair of the heart, being subject to worldly conditions, is no different. A love between two persons can grow into something deep and matured, fed by selfless giving, mutual respect and sharing. It can also turn sour when the parties involved become careless with one another or when conditions change through no one's fault.

One way to find solace for your mental agony or frustration is to understand the degree of your own sufferings and difficulties with that experienced by others. You think that everything around you is about to collapse. However, if you try to take a mental stock of things and try to count your blessings, you will find, surprisingly, that you are better off than many others who suffer more. In short, you have been unduly exaggerating your problems. Many others are worse off than you and yet they do not worry unduly.

Another method to reduce your problems is to recapitulate what you have gone through before, under similar or worse circumstances and how you have, through your patience and efforts, been able to surmount your then seemingly difficulties. By doing so, you will not permit your existing problems to 'drown you'. On the contrary you will determine to resolve whatever issues or problems that may be facing you. You should realise that you have gone through worse situations and that you are prepared to face the issue – come what may. With this frame of mind, you will soon regain your self-confidence and will be able to face and resolve whatever problems that are in store for you.

22

HAPPY MARRIED LIFE

Some believe that marriages are made in heaven. But when marriages are badly handled, they could just as well have been made in hell.

In a marriage, both the husband and wife must think more of the partnership than they do of themselves. This partnership is an interweaving of interests, and sacrifices will have to be made for the sake of both parties. It is from mutual understanding and concern that security and contentment in marriage can be established.

There are no short-cuts to happiness in marriage. No two human beings can possibly live together in an intimate emotional relationship for a long period of time without having some misunderstanding or friction from time to time. Understanding and tolerance are required to overcome the feelings of jealousy, anger and suspicion. To think that one does not need to adopt a give-and-take attitude is to presume that love in marriage is just for the asking without any sacrifice on our part.

Building a Successful Marriage

Success in marriage is based on compatibility rather than just only finding the right partner. Both partners must try to be the right person by acting out of mutual respect, love and concern for each other. Love is an inner feeling and a fulfilment arising from the mutual healthy growth with and for the other person. In a successful marriage, a partner must not always try to get things his or her own way. This brings to mind a humourous saying – *'Man has his will but woman has her way'*. There is only one path to be trodden by both, it may be uneven, bumpy and sometimes difficult, but it is always a 'mutual path'.

A happy marriage is not one in which we are to exist with eyes closed. We see faults as well as virtues, and we should accept the fact that no one is perfect. A husband and wife must learn to share the happiness and pain in their daily lives. Mutual understanding is the secret formula of a happy marriage. Marriage is a blessing, but unfortunately, many people treat it otherwise due to a lack of correct communication and understanding.

Most of the marital troubles and worries which normally arise are due to an unwillingness of one partner to compromise and to practise patience with the other. The golden rule to avoid a minor misunderstanding being blown out of proportion is to practise patience, tolerance and understanding. Human beings are emotional and hence are liable to get into tantrums which lead them to be angry. Husbands and wives should do their utmost for both not to be angry at the same time. This is the golden rule for a happy married life. If both parties are not angry at the same time, problems can easily be resolved by adopting the noble spirit of patience, tolerance and understanding.

The husband should treat his wife with respect, understanding and consideration and not as a servant nor as a doll in his hands. Although he may be regarded as the bread-winner of the family, it is also his duty to help his wife with the household work whenever he is free. The wife, on the other hand, should not always nag or grumble at her husband over trivial matters. If he really has certain shortcomings, she should try to talk with him and correct him in a gentle manner. A spouse should try to tolerate and handle many things without bothering the partner, especially when there are problems affecting one's career. If one is inclined towards jealousy, one must try to restrain suspicions over the partner's movements since they may not at all be justifiable. In

Buddhism, mutual respect and trust are of paramount importance in a happy union.

Sex in Marriage

Sex should be given its due place in a happy marriage. Like fire, sex is a good servant but can be a bad master. It should neither be unhealthily repressed nor morbidly exaggerated. The desire for sex, like any other emotion, must be regulated by reason. Although it is an important element in the happiness of most married couples, it is necessary to realise that one can be happy without giving sex a paramount role. On the other hand, one can have a good sex life and still be unhappy. Real love is not just physical: it is a spiritual communion, a meeting of minds.

Sex is much more than the physical gratification of desires. It is the basis for an intimate life-long companionship. Down through the ages, love and mutual respect have been shown to be the basis for close intimacy between the sexes. Dr. Helen Kaplan of Cornell Medical Center says that without intimacy there can be no real love. Her definition of intimacy is the sharing of feelings, not information. Couples who are not intimate will tend to talk of frivolous subjects like the weather, the latest TV shows or what to eat for dinner. They never make it a point to let each other know if they are really happy, unhappy, frightened, worried or any other such intimate feelings. They are also not interested to know how their partner really feels.

The married couple should make every effort to cultivate the timeless virtues of chastity, fidelity and decency. Real growth only comes through the development of these virtues. None can repeal the cosmic moral law of cause and effect, of the lasting unity of all human beings. The hope of personal growth and harmony in society lies in the recognition of this basic law, rather than surrendering oneself to base and coarse animal instincts which only bring suffering to those whom we dearly love. Self respect, human dignity or humane qualities are eroding in modern society.

******

Who are more civilised? The traditional way of dressing among the women of a hill tribe was to leave the upper part of their bodies bare. They did not draw any attention among their men who went about their daily duties as they had been doing for generations. However, when they were about to be visited by some officials undertaking a study on their way of life, the young girls were told by their chieftain to hide themselves. They were safe among the men of their tribe, but there was no telling what the so called educated men from the civilized world would do to them.

******

The tendency of people today towards an overdependency and obsession with sex can be a cause for alarm. Our forefathers erected a veil of secrecy and hypocrisy around the subject, and it is well that the veil has for the most part been torn down. But when sex becomes glorified and sensationalised like the way it is done today, it hinders the development of higher values in society. The mass media particularly has exploited the erotic side of life so enticingly and successfully that humanity is bombarded sick by a ceaseless barrage of sexual stimulation from every side. The way how they organise their way of life is to show others that the sex life is the most important aspect in human life and to neglect all the other important duties and responsibilities.

Having a Good Marriage

The Buddha says that a marriage between a bad husband and a bad wife is like a dead body existing with another dead body. Marriage between a bad man and a good woman is like a dead body, existing with an angel. Married life between a good man and a bad woman is like an angel living with a dead body. Married life between a good man and a good woman is like an angel living with another angel. Montaigne jokes about married life by saying: '*A good marriage would be between a blind wife and deaf husband.*' (The wife will not see the man's weaknesses and the husband will not hear her nagging.)

According to a certain religion, a man may marry more than one wife, while other religions restrict marriage to one man and one wife. As far as Buddhism is concerned, marriage is a matter of personal choice, and people are also subject to the laws of the country they live in. Even in countries where polygamy is permissible, there is enough evidence to show that a man having more than one wife will only invite more worries and burdens throughout his life.

Most of us already have more than enough troubles. Instead of overcoming them many people go out looking for some more troubles.

******

One head and two wives. There was once an elderly man who was not satisfied with the one wife to whom he had been married for some years. He decided to take on a second wife who was charming and beautiful. Now, this second wife felt rather embarrassed to be seen with such an old man. So in order to make him look young, she spent a lot of time plucking out all the grey hairs that had appeared on his head. When his first wife noticed this, she began to pull out his black hairs one by one, hoping to make him appear older. This contest between the two of them went on and in the end, the man became completely bald, with neither a single grey hair nor black hair on his head.

******

Ladies attach a lot of importance to birthdays and anniversaries. Caring husbands should remember these dates and should never be too busy to keep love alive with little tributes and attention. Little acts of attention such as these show the person you love that you are thinking of her, that you want to please her, that her happiness and welfare are very near and dear to your heart. Wives do appreciate such little acts of attention such as these from their courteous husbands and it is this life long goodwill that keeps the home fires burning. Little acts of love such as these are at the bottom of most marital happiness.

Married couples today can regulate the size of their family through proper family planning. Wise couples should plan their families according to their incomes and capabilities. There is no reason for Buddhists to oppose contraception and the practice of birth control which prevent the fertilization of the ovum. However, once the embryo is formed, it must be allowed to take its full course during the pregnancy. Buddhism does not support nor condone the act of abortion which constitutes an act of killing.

'Marriage resembles a pair of scissors joined together so that they cannot be separated. Often they move in opposite directions. But woe betide anyone who comes between them'

'The chain of wedlock is so heavy that it takes two to carry it'

Readers wishing further information on this subject, are advised to read the book 'A Happy Married Life' by the same author.

23

YOUR BEAUTY

Beauty is very subjective. What you consider beautiful may be ugly to another.

Advertisements play a key role in influencing our concept of beauty. Beauty is how we see it, as the saying goes – 'beauty is in the eyes of the beholder'. Aggressive promotional tactics are used to shape people's expectations as well as revolutionise accepted levels of style, quality and glamour. Over time they have managed to develop these unrealistic expectations to such a degree that make conceited men and women the world over demand beauty as a basic human right. And the so called beauty which many people seek are external rather than internal. External good looks are what they look for when selecting friends or when choosing a life partner.

Because of the high premium being placed on good looks, people try various methods to achieve this desirable state. It could mean going for aerobics, an intensive slimming course, a face lift, wearing fashionable clothes, a new hairdo, or makeup. Usually, ladies and also some men, tend to be very conscious and particular about their weight when they discover that they have put on a few extra pounds.

While males are not exempt from this fad, it is generally true to say that the fairer sex will go to great lengths to look and feel beautiful. The womenfolk in modern society spend a good part of their income on expensive clothes and cosmetics. Their choice of what to buy is heavily influenced and dictated by the expensive promotional gimmicks adopted by fashion houses and cosmetic companies.

It is indeed surprising how profoundly women are interested in clothes. For example, if a man and woman meet another man and woman on the street, the woman seldom looks at the other man: she usually looks to see how well the other woman is dressed.

Despite all their seriousness in the search for beauty, people have forgotten to use a source everyone is endowed with by nature but not often used. They miss out on this natural source of beauty. Maybe this source has easily been overlooked because present day cosmetics provide a convenient substitute to give an instant though false conception of real beauty. In this age of fast foods and all sorts of 'instant this' and 'instant that' many women resort to instant beauty aids and cosmetics which are readily available in the market. Now coming back to our natural source of beauty, we like to ask: What can this source of beauty be? None other than kindness, love, simplicity and the beauty of the heart. Of all the cosmetics available, the best is loving kindness. It is natural, inexpensive and always effective. The one who has this quality looks beautiful even without having to worry about what is applied on the face or done to the hair.

Even if one is born with plain looks, one can look radiant and attractive if the virtues of love, kindness and patience are cultivated. These virtues will give rise to an internal charm that will radiate outwards, making that person irresistible. Many people will be attracted to him or her because of that special charm as beauty naturally exudes from the person's body. Unlike external physical beauty which fades like a flower, this internal beauty has an aura of charm which can often become more intense in its glow the more mature the person becomes.

On the other hand, even if a person is born handsome and with beautiful features, many people will be turned away from such a person if he or she is jealous, selfish, cunning and conceited. But if the person is overflowing with loving-kindness, speaks gently and politely, he or she will be far more attractive than the so-called beautiful person who is conceited and full of pride. A beautiful complexion can attract attention, but for how long? There is no complexion which can remain beautiful especially if the person's mind is corrupted. External beauty will soon fade like all things must. The saying that *'beauty is but skin deep'* is indeed very true. But the beauty of loving kindness remains, and is appreciated by all alike.

The world is like a mirror. If we look at the mirror with a smiling face, we will see a face smiling back at us. But if we look at it with a frown or a face of anger, we will also see the same ugly face reflected back. In the same way, if we were to act with kindness and sympathy, the same good qualities will be returned to us. And when we perform noble virtues which arise in the heart, they will be translated into good speech and deeds which are apparent to all.

If one is born good looking, one should consider oneself to be fortunate. To be born beautiful or hand-some is a blessing according to the Buddha. But one should not, on account of that beauty, or handsome-ness develop arrogance or conceit. It will only make such a person repulsive to others. Not only will that conceit work against a person's appearance, but more importantly, it will be an obstacle to one's spiritual progress and happiness.

24

ACCUMULATION OF WEALTH

It is not wrong to be rich if such gains are obtained through rightful means.

After many days of heavy rains, a village which was known for its good swimmers became flooded when the river burst its banks. When the rain ceased, five or six friends in the village decided to take a boat to the opposite bank. Just as they were in the middle of the river, the boat started to fall apart. Since all of them could swim very well, they jumped into the river and started swimming across to the other bank. One of the friends was found to be swimming very slowly despite using all his strength.

'Hey, why are you falling behind?' his friends shouted. 'You used to swim better than the rest of us.'

'I have a thousand coins tied round my waist and they are very heavy!'

'The water is swift and the current is strong. Take the coins off and throw them away!' they admonished him.

Despite his exhaustion, he shook his head because he could not bear to part with his money.

Some of his friends who climbed onto the far shore saw that he was sinking fast. 'Throw away the money!' they shouted again. 'Why must you be so stupid? You are about to sink!'

But he still hung on to the money, and was soon swept away by the swift river and drowned.

Contentment

No one can reach the state of perfect happiness unless he brings his covetous heart and mind under complete control. So long as he seeks his happiness in the satisfaction of his desire for material gains, he will never find it. It will be just an elusive dream. It is humanly impossible to obtain everything one wishes, since insatiability is the very nature of craving.

Clinging to Money

The religion of the materialistic world today is deifying money. Everybody wants to be rich quickly, at all costs and by any means available, whether by rightful or wrongful methods. The world is so caught up with accumulating wealth that the honourable virtues of morality, honesty, and integrity seem to have lost their influence and meaning on humanity. Under the siege of materialism, humanity is rapidly losing sight of spiritual values. It is not wrong to be rich, if such gains are obtained through rightful means. Ill-gotten gains, however, will lead to problems, difficulties and a guilty conscience.

In his pursuit of wealth, man has lost sight of the fact that money is merely a means to an end. He has failed to understand the nature, meaning and purpose of wealth. He is only interested in one aim – just to have more money. As a result, he ends up in a blind alley frustrated and confused because he is no nearer to true happiness than when he was poor. This is the reason why some rich men are unhappy, restless and miserable because they fail to understand that money might be able to buy them sensual and mundane pleasures but not happiness.

Many cases of swindling, cheating, and fraud have been reported in the newspapers involving billions of dollars. These heinous acts have caused untold suffering and even death to those unable to bear their losses physically or mentally. These despicable acts are committed by those holding responsible positions. They misuse their intelligence and the trust placed in them by dishonestly enriching themselves at the expense of others.

Such unfortunate dishonesty and breach of trust are

the result of the obsessive preoccupation with getting rich as quickly as possible. Their sole aim in life is to make money, and more money, and they are indifferent even to religious admonitions. Honesty and integrity mean nothing to them. They need more money for more enjoyment of their senses and desire for possession.

The Faulty Equation

We cannot deny the fact that accumulation of wealth does bring some degree of happiness and security. But we should not make the accumulation of wealth the sole purpose of our lives, as is happening now, and forget that there are many more things to make life meaningful than just the acquisition of wealth. To maintain peace and harmony in our lives, we must adopt a realistic and reasonable attitude towards wealth.

> *He who knows that enough is enough will always have enough.*
>
> ~ *Lao Tse* ~

Everybody seeks happiness, and it is quite natural to do so. Unfortunately, many people equate happiness with wealth. To a wise man, this is a false equation. To have but few desires and satisfaction with simple things is a sign of a superior man. All great men led simple, yet dignified lives, practising self-restraint and avoiding all those excesses which encourage sensuality and dissipate vital energy. To put it another way, the fewer the necessities, the greater the happiness. Epicurus, the Greek philosopher says, *'If you want to make a man happy, add not to his riches but take away his desires.'*

Wealth and prosperity are not the only way to achieve happiness, since the perpetually and singularly discontented mind cannot be satisfied by mere physical comfort. Most of our daily needs can be quite easily met, but not our insatiable desires. In fact a person who could simplify his wants can get a great deal more out of his life. Man's body needs very little for its upkeep. Many people tend to eat too much especially if they can afford it. They live to eat, not eat to live. We need not have to spend a lot to clothe ourselves decently. As Socrates once said: *'Good food and rich clothes, all possible luxuries, are what you call happiness, but I believe that a state of being where one wishes for nothing is the greatest of all bliss. To be able to approach the greatest happiness, one must get used to being satisfied with little.'*

Using Wealth Properly

Wealth should be used well and wisely. It is to be used for your welfare as well as others. If a person spends his time clinging to his property, without fulfilling his obligations towards his country, people and religion, he will lead an empty life plagued with worries.

Finally, when the time comes for him to leave this world, he will realise too late that he had not made full use of his wealth. No one, including himself, has really benefited from the wealth he had so painstakingly accumulated.

The Buddha has advised us against the foolishness of clinging on selfishly to our property, without attempting to improve the quality of life and happiness of others. *Your property will remain when you die. Your friends and relatives will follow you up to your grave. But only your good and bad actions which you have done during your life-time will accompany you beyond the grave.*

Man has the potential to do good or commit evil. However, with deceit a person is able to twist and turn matters to his advantage in order to justify any dishonest and unethical act he may commit. When any bad act is committed, it is better to call a spade a spade and admit wrong doing to oneself. Otherwise, one will continue to be chained to the evils of unsatisfactoriness. Even Mussolini and Hitler claimed they had good motives when they caused the sufferings of others. So would a tigress, when she carries away a child to feed her cubs. If you want to be truly happy, you must clearly examine your actions to determine that they are not motivated by self interest but for the welfare of all beings. It is time, therefore, that we take a fresh survey of our situation and reexamine anew the values we hold.

Perhaps this poem by an unknown author can help

us to have a better understanding of the value of money.

What Money Can Buy

A bed but not sleep
Books but not knowledge
Food but not appetite
Finery but not beauty
A house but not a home
Medicine but not health
Luxuries but not comfort
Pleasures but not happiness
Religion but not salvation.

Say not that this is yours and that is mine,
Just say, this came to you and to me;
So we may not regret the fading shine,
Of all the glorious things which ceased to be.

25

LIVING IN HARMONY WITH OTHERS

Living in harmony with others means living in harmony with nature. And nature itself protects you.

An important factor for a happy life is the ability to live in harmony with others. To achieve this, we must recognise that there are many paths people can take to reach the same goal. Therefore, we should not be unduly upset if other people practise their own customs or have opinions which are different from ours.

Manners and Customs

The standard of good manners differ among people

belonging to different societies. In some countries, guests at dinner are expected to eat as noisily as possible. It is also not considered impolite if the guests belch at the end of the meal since this would indicate to the host that they had really enjoyed the meal. Eating rice and curries by using the fingers is looked down upon by some people. To some others eating rice and curries using a fork and spoon is like carrying on a romantic relationship through an interpreter. Such table manners would be considered rude, ill-mannered in other societies. While in one country, putting one's finger in one's mouth or nose for any reason is considered most insulting, it may mean nothing in some other countries. Some people think it is degrading to be struck by a shoe, yet among other people, a slipper can be used for spanking a child.

We discover the peculiarities of the manners and customs prevailing in other societies most noticeably when travelling. We should not prejudge manners and custom too quickly as to what is proper or improper. In themselves, manners are neither good nor bad, but when they cause ill feelings in others, then this can be considered as bad manners.

We are living in an ever changing world. We should not cling blindly to the traditions, customs, manners rites and rituals practised by our forefathers or ancestors who adopted these practices according to their beliefs and understanding capacity prevalent at that time. Some customs or traditions handed down by our ancestors may be good, while others are less useful. We should consider with an open mind whether these practices are congenial and significant to the modern world.

In the Kalama Sutta, the Buddha has given this advice about customs, traditions, beliefs and practices: 'When you know for yourself that certain things are unwholesome [akusala] and wrong, and bad for you and others, then give them up ... And when you know for yourselves that certain things are wholesome [kusala] and good for you and others, then accept them and follow them.'

Some elderly people cannot tolerate the modern ideas and ways of living of the younger generation. They expect their children to follow the same age old customs and traditions of their forefathers. Instead of adopting such an attitude, they should allow the children to move with the times if the activities are harmless. Elders should call to mind how their own parents had objected to certain popular modes of behaviour prevalent at the time when they were young. These differences in perception between the conservative parents and the younger generation is a common source of conflict within families of today. This does not mean that parents should hesitate to counsel and guide their children if they have gone astray due to some erroneous values. But when correcting them, they should observe the principle that prevention is better than punishment. Parents should also explain to their children why they disapprove or approve of certain values.

Allowing Others the Right to Differ

If a person lives all by himself, then he will not have any problem with differing opinions. But if we have chosen to live in society, we must learn to respect and deal with views and opinions of others even though they do not conform with ours.

U Thant, the former Secretary General of the United Nations has said that when he was in his office he took great care not to push his personal beliefs and traditional practices on those he worked with either by example or speech. When he was at home however, he followed his Burmese traditions concerning language, food and religion fully. This shows how at least one great man never used his personal influence to force others to accept his own belief and way of life.

We are also living in a world where might is stronger than right. The strong takes advantage of the weak and the rich exploits the poor. We should avoid acting in this way. If we cannot agree, we have to learn at least to agree to disagree. We should express our views gently and politely without trying to impose views on others by force. Those who use physical force to overcome their opponents clearly show their inability to convince the opponents that they are right.

We find comfort in those who agree with us, but personal growth occurs in situations where there are differences in views. Sometimes the opinion others have of our attitudes or actions may not be something

we would like to hear. But if we listen to them carefully, we will realise that there are some truths in those
opinions. This can give us a chance for self improvement if we are prepared to change our ways and
approaches. The world is like a garden with different
kinds of flowers. Like a bee gathering honey from a
flower, we should be selective in choosing what is
good and leave behind what is not useful. It is impossible for us to please everybody when we want to
do something, because different people have different
opinions on one particular issue.

* * * * * *

We cannot please everybody. Once a man and his son
were taking a donkey to the market. As they were
walking, some people saw them and remarked, 'Look
at these fools, why don't they ride the donkey?' The
man heard this and asked the son to ride the donkey
while he walked alongside. An old woman seeing this
remarked, 'What is the world coming to? Look at that
young man riding comfortably while he makes his
poor father walk!' So the young man got down and
this time the father rode the donkey. As they went
along, a young woman passing by said, 'Why don't
both of you get on the animal?' So they listened to her
and both rode on the animal. Yet another group who
saw them said, 'Oh! What a poor animal. It has to
carry those two fat good-for-nothings! How cruel
some people can be!' By this time the father and son

were getting quite fed up. They decided to dismount and carry the donkey instead so as to stop everyone from talking. This led people to laugh and say, 'look at these human "donkeys" carrying a donkey'. Of course the donkey did not like this peculiar arrangement at all. Whilst approaching a river, it struggled vigorously to set itself free and finally the man, his son and their donkey all landed themselves in the water.

******

When you try and please everyone, you will end up pleasing no one and in the end, you will only land yourself in trouble.

Patience and Tolerance

Those who can remain cheerful during difficult times are admirable and a source of inspiration to others. They can avoid conflicts by seeing the lighter side of things. A wise man can avoid a quarrel by answering jokes and remarks directed at him with another joke.

When people humiliate us we must learn how to face them gently by good humouredly turning the joke against them.

******

A joke for the Joker. Once there was a famous Englishman who went to a party. When he was out of the room, his friends decided to play a practical joke on him. They painted the face of an ass on the back of his overcoat. The party ended and as the man went to get his coat, he noticed the painting. Instead of getting angry, he calmly asked, 'Did anyone wipe his face on my coat this evening?' His friends of course were surprised at this question. He explained, 'Well, I just asked because the impression of his face remains on the back of my coat.'

******

What should you do when you lose in a game? You should not show your temper, since by doing so you will not only spoil the fun of the game but also lose your friends' respect.

Every person is responsible for making a better world by planting the seeds of patience, love and honesty deeply in the human heart. Eventually, a new era will blossom during his lifetime bringing benefit to his generation and the generations to come. He is a cultured man who knows how to face difficulties with sympathy and understanding.

The mark of a great man lies in how he faces daily irritations with equanimity.

******

He is not my servant but my teacher. A great Indian Buddhist teacher Ven. Dipankara was invited to Tibet to preach the Dhamma. The teacher took along with him a man who was not only quarrelsome and irresponsible but a bad cook as well. After observing him for quite some time the Tibetans approached the teacher respectfully and said, 'Master, why do you tolerate this useless cook of yours – he is more of a nuisance than a help to you. Why don't you send him back? We will gladly attend to your needs.' The teacher smiled and replied, 'Ah! you don't understand, I do not keep him as my servant but as my teacher.' The Tibetans were surprised and asked 'How is that so?' The teacher explained, 'You see, his inefficiency and his quarrelsome nature teach me to practise patience and tolerance everyday. Therefore, I value him.'

******

Some may say that the quality of patience and tolerance is impractical and too idealistic to be followed. Some are cynical and wonder if man who is struggling to eke out a living from a hostile world can really be interested in cultivating love and kindness. While it is not easy to practise these qualities, they are possible with perseverance and determination. The Buddha and his disciples proved this to be true on numerous occasions.

Diplomacy

You cannot hope to achieve peace by correcting each and every person in this world. In the same way, you cannot remove the world of stones and thorns so that the pathway may be smooth. To feel comfortable walking on uneven ground, we should try wearing a pair of shoes instead. Likewise, we should learn to guard our senses to have peace of mind since we cannot succeed in removing disturbing objects from the world.

There are many ways to correct a person if he is wrong. By criticising, blaming and shouting at him publicly, you will not be able to correct him but you only make him more adamant in his views.

Speak to him kindly in pointing out his mistakes, he is more likely to listen to you, and some day he will thank you for your guidance and kindness.

Whenever you express your views regarding certain matters, avoid harsh words spoken with anger so as not to hurt the feelings of others. Always express your views gently or politely. On the other hand, you should not lose your temper or show your sulky face when your faults are pointed out. You may think that by losing your temper, showing an ugly face, and shouting at others, you can intimidate others in order that they may overlook your shortcomings. This is a wrong attitude to adopt. Rudeness, yelling, anger and swearing are a weak man's imitation of strength.

H. H. the Dalai Lama once said: 'When I meet another human being, I would never consider about his race, colour, creed or status in life. What I would feel is that I have met another member of our human family'.

To know more about human problems read 'Whither Mankind?' by the same author.

26

MAN CAN CHANGE HIS ENVIRONMENT

Mind is the architect of our fate. It can make us sick, or it can cure us.

Nature is evenly balanced; her equilibrium cannot be disturbed. Natural laws, which operate unerringly and inexorably, are not swayed by praises, prayers or sacrifices. They operate at the physical and mental realms without the intervention of a law-giver. One of such natural laws which have a strong bearing on the quality of human life is the cosmic law of kamma. This law operates at the moral sphere. Wholesome and unwholesome acts performed by thought, word and deed will in due time produce their corresponding good and bad results.

If a man is cruel, performs wicked acts, and does not live in conformity with the natural cosmic laws, he pollutes the whole atmosphere with his unwholesome deeds. As a result of such unwholesome deeds, unfavourable results will arise making it difficult for him to lead a happy, contented and peaceful life. He creates unhappiness for himself and others with his polluted mind. On the other hand, if he lives in conformity with the natural cosmic law and leads a righteous and blameless life, he purifies the atmosphere with the merits of his virtues. With his positive mental vibrations, he influences those around him as well as creates an environment conducive to peace and happiness.

Cultivating Virtue

But virtue and a positive frame of mind are not qualities which arise in a person automatically. For many, it is so easy to give in to anger, jealousy, ill will, vengeance, selfishness, especially when under pressure or competition. Effort is needed for a person to return good in the face of unfavourable conditions. He needs a clear appreciation of the importance of practising virtue and the need to overcome hatred, egoistic pride and selfish desires.

****

What is real treasure? Once there was a man who loved to flatter others for his personal gain. He obtained a piece of jade one day and tried to present it to a minister. Despite persuasions, the minister refused to accept the jade.

The man said, 'This is a real treasure! No ordinary person is worthy of using it. Only a person of your calibre can use it. It is only appropriate that this piece of jade be owned and worn by you.'

'You may consider this jade to be a treasure,' said the upright minister. 'But I am not easily taken in by flattery. This is my treasure!'

******

Virtue is cultivated through conscientious training. A person who wishes to acquire virtues should make it a habit to cultivate moral qualities in daily life. In the same manner a student must work on his lessons consistently in order to be successful in his studies. In the beginning, he has to draw on every effort and determination to develop positive qualities, especially if he has a strong inclination towards negative tendencies. Through the application of mindfulness and effort, he can reverse these negative tendencies and cultivate good mental, verbal and bodily habits. Once these good habits are in place and developed through practice, a time will come when he will find it increasingly difficult to commit negative and unwholesome actions. The actions that arise from him will naturally be spontaneous, creative and skilful, good thought habits, lead to happiness.

Using the Mind Creatively

Mind is the almighty, all-powerful, the omnipotent creator of good and evil. Mind is the cause of all evils, and all evils are mind-made. It can also be the cause of all happiness, prosperity and pleasure, for all these states are mind-made. Is it not amazing that though our mind is within us, yet we do not know its nature? But some people claim that they can read the minds of others. No one can see the future, least of all one's own.

******

Reading others' minds. A professional mind-reader was making a fortune by claiming that he was able to read the thoughts of other people. One day a young man came to him. He showed him a big stick and said, 'Read my mind. Am I going to beat you or not?' The mind-reader saw the predicament he was in. The young man would deny it if he said either yes or no. Being unable to read the young man's mind, the mind reader saw that it was best to say nothing.

******

The Buddha did not regard evil as something to be atoned for through a saviour, but a defilement arising from ignorance which has to be outgrown through wisdom. He rejected as a theological fiction the belief that man is cursed by a God, born in sin, shaped in iniquity, and destined to a miserable eternity. In the view of the Enlightened One, every person has the capacity for the pursuit of goodness, and even the most vicious person can by his or her own effort become a most virtuous being. And any crime, however great, is not punishable by an unending eternity of suffering.

Think of the mind as a tool. It can be constructive if used well, or destructive if used badly. The choice is up to us. A single thought can set off a chain reaction of deeds that can either bring happiness or sadness in its path. It is for this reason that so much emphasis is placed on mind training in Buddhism, since a well-trained mind is clearly the key to a happy, peaceful and contented life.

The mind is somewhat like electricity. The electric current can kill a person who grasps a live wire just as readily as it will flood his home with light. So much depends on how it is used. Similarly, a person who performs evil deeds and ignores the law of the mind is only inviting suffering. Conversely, the mastery of his mind can bring him great happiness.

The Buddha says: *'Radiant is the mind; pure energy is its essence. It is polluted only by defilements.'* It is not easy to control our evil thoughts, and even more difficult to renounce unwholesome thoughts of lust, hate and delusion, which can only be eradicated through mind training.

Thoughts are behind our every action. The repeated performance of these actions in turn determine our character. If we think kindly, we become kind; if we think cruelly, we become cruel; if we think deceitfully, we become deceitful; if we think honestly, we become honest; and if we think compassionately, we become compassionate. Such is the effect of our thoughts on our behaviour and nature.

Our Mission

It is, therefore, important for us to develop our thoughts of compassion and wisdom so as to develop our humane qualities. We should be happy to be born as human beings. Being born human is the result of our past good actions. As humans, we have the unparalleled opportunity to acquire merits and develop wisdom, thereby contributing to our well-being and happiness. Let us live a life filled with purpose and add quality to human existence. We should not waste our human birth by abusing this privilege and committing unwholesome actions which surely lead to misery. Do not let our days pass by like the shadow of a cloud, leaving no trace behind.

What is needed today is the return to the wisdom of the past, which is also the highest wisdom of the future. Yet it is not just the wisdom of the past or the future. It is the eternal wisdom discovered by the Buddha and it belongs to all ages and all races of mankind. It is the wisdom of the Dhamma. This wisdom is like a deep well, fed by perennial springs. Let us draw from this perennial spring of wisdom for without it, lasting peace and real progress for individuals as well as nations will be impossible.

27

HUMAN DIGNITY

It has been clearly mentioned in the ancient philosophy that the purpose of our life is not just selfish aggrandizement but the noble act of being of service to others.

Let us try to ascertain to what extent we are able to discuss, .from the Buddhist point of view, that which is relevant to this simple and yet sometimes confusing subject touching on human dignity.

What are the humane qualities which give rise to dignity and nobility? They are based on the moral, ethical, intellectual and spiritual norms which we human beings uphold and treasure in our day-to-day relationships with one another. As human beings we have minds which we can develop to such an extent that we can differentiate between what is right and what is wrong, between what we should be proud of and what we should be ashamed of. These are humane qualities that we all cherish as human beings. It is in cherishing such values that we distinguish ourselves as human beings and not animals.

To be able to develop one's mind one must be able to develop and sustain one's thinking power which is the ability to judge between what is ethical and what is unethical, what is moral and immoral, what is good and what is bad and what is right and what is wrong. These are attributes within the grasp of human beings. Animals do not have such attributes – animals act by instinct. It would appear that human beings are the only living beings that can develop their minds or their thinking power to such high levels – even to the extent of attaining Buddhahood.

Moral Shame and Moral Fear

Before the advent of world religions, human beings were guided by two valuable factors, which in primitive times, contributed to the upholding of the dignity of man. They are *'Hiri'* and *'Ottappa'*. *'Hiri'* is the shame a pure mind feels at the thought of doing evil. *'Ottappa'* is the aversion which causes one to shrink from doing evil. 'Moral shame' and 'Moral fear' invariably govern all actions of the human being. The animal is guided only by the instinct of survival, and does not act through a sense of morality. However, when human beings succumb to the evil effects of drugs, liquor, lust, anger, greed, envy, selfishness and hate, they lose their balance. They deny themselves the right to human dignity and become like animals.

While we pride ourselves as civilised human beings, we note with deep regret the behaviour and attitudes of some of our people which can be described as no better than those of animals. This is certainly not a development that we want to encourage for mankind. A human being who is worthy of respect, should be one who has the attributes of Fear and Shame, who is kind, compassionate and sympathetic to others, who is afraid to cause harm to others but is ever prepared to lend a helping hand when in need. These are ordinary human values which we should all cherish and uphold. We should develop our humane qualities and not violate them. By being of service to others, we develop great virtues which are inherent in us. By being of service to others, we show a spirit of understanding, kindness, compassion, honesty, simplicity, gentleness, humility and contentment. These are worthy human values which we should be proud to acquire.

Different Characteristics of Human Beings

There are certain characteristics in our human nature which we have to guard and nurture carefully into useful human values. Roughly speaking, these characteristics are divided into three aspects, our *animal* nature, our *human* nature and our *divine* nature.

These three characteristics influence our behaviour in various degrees. If we give way to our *animal nature* without making any effort to subdue or control our ugly actions, we will become a liability to society. Religion is an important tool which can help us to control our animal nature. Religion, with the noble teachings coming from illustrious religious leaders, should serve as a guide for proper humane behaviour. Religion also serves as a tool for us to cultivate, nurture and improve on the various aspects of our hidden *human nature*. By cultivating and improving our human nature, we ultimately achieve our divine goal – we attain our *divine nature*. By achieving divine nature, we achieve the level of development at which the base emotions of greed, lust, anger, hatred, jealousy, envy and other unwelcome attributes are completely eliminated, thus making the human being more noble and worthy of the highest respect. With the help of religion, we control and subdue our animal nature, we cultivate and improve our human nature, and we achieve our divine nature.

This divine nature depends on the development of goodwill or friendliness or care for the welfare of others, compassion or kindness, sympathetic joy at others' progress and impartiality towards gain or loss and praise or blame. This is also known as the sublime state.

It is ironical that many religionists are still under the misapprehension that one can achieve one's divine goal by the simple act of praying or worshipping and the simple performance of certain rites and rituals. This attitude must be changed. We have our duties and obligations to fulfill in order that we may live as real and dignified human beings. We have to cultivate and develop our human nature in order to achieve our divine attributes. We must practise all the human values for the good and well-being of humanity. We must do all the good we can and eradicate all that is evil. The religions of the world have been developed to guide us and show us the correct path to live in peace and harmony. All religions should provide their followers with important and suitable guidelines to enable everyone to live and work together with mutual respect, understanding and dignity. As co-religionists we should all be able to live with one another without harbouring any hatred, jealousy, enmity or feelings of superiority. Buddhism gives us such guidance.

One of the golden rules to lead a dignified life is to have a balanced livelihood – without in any way going into extremes. The Buddha does not advise us to torture our body or our mind in the cause of religion. We can practise our religion as rational beings. Do not overdo things. Should not forget the most important aspect of life – our spiritual development. The teaching of the Buddha can be categorised in three ways: happiness for this life, happiness for the hereafter and happiness for the ultimate achievement – Nibbana. In the pursuit of these three kinds of happiness, a man can achieve dignity and nobility.

With bad advisors forever left behind,
From paths of evil he departs for eternity,
Soon to see the Buddha of Limitless Light
And perfect Samantabhadra's Supreme Vows.

The supreme and endless blessings
of Samantabhadra's deeds,
I now universally transfer.
May every living being, drowning and adrift,
Soon return to the Land of
Limitless Light!

The Vows of Samantabhadra

I vow that when my life approaches its end,
All obstructions will be swept away;
I will see Amitabha Buddha,
And be born in his Land of Ultimate Bliss and Peace.

When reborn in the Western Land,
I will perfect and completely fulfill
Without exception these Great Vows,
To delight and benefit all beings.

The Vows of Samantabhadra
Avatamsaka Sutra

PLACES TO CONTACT AND ORDER

AUSTRALIA
PURE LAND LEARNING COLLEGE
ASSOCIATION INC.
PURE LAND TRAINING ASSOCIATION
INC. 淨宗學院
57 WEST STREET TOOWOOMBA,
QUEENSLAND 4350 AUSTRALIA
TEL: 61-7-46378765 ; FAX: 61-7-46378764
E-mail:purelandcollege@yahoo.com.au

CANADA
AMITABHA BUDDHIST ASSOCIATION
(MONTREAL),
2903 MADELEIN DANSEREAU
MONTREAL PQ CANADA H1Y 3J6
TEL:514-5256846; FAX:514-5256846;
Email: wanhuaxu@hotmail.com

ENGLAND
THE MIDLANDS INTERNATIONAL
BUDDHIST ASSOCIATION IN THE U.K.
23, WEYCROFT ROAD, PERRY
COMMON, BIRMINGHAM, B23 5AD,
UK
TEL:44-121-3827108 ;
FAX: 44-121-3848333 ;
Email: mibauk86@hotmail.com

INDIA
MAHA BODHI SOCIETY
14, KALIDASA ROAD, GANDHINAGAR,
BANGALORE-560 009, INDIA
TEL: 91-80-22250684, 91-812-260684;
FAX:91-80-22264438, 91-80-22250292
Email: mahabodhi@vsnl.com ;
bodhi@bgl.vsnl.net.in

INDONESIA
YAYASAN DHARMA RANGSI,
BUDDHIST EDUCATION AND
TRAINING CENTER,
JL. RAYA DARMO PERMAI III, PLAZA
SEGI DELAPAN, BLOK C NO. 801-802,
SURBAYA, INDONESIA
TEL:62-31-7345143 ; FAX: 62-31-7345143

MALAYSIA
PERSATUAN PENGANUT AGAMA
BUDDHA AMITABHA (MALAYSIA),
16-A, FIRST FLOOR, JLN PAHANG
53000 KUALA LUMPUR, MALAYSIA
TEL: 60-3-40414101; 60-3-40452630;
FAX: 60-3-40412172
Email: amtbmy@pd.jaring.my

PHILIPPINES
UNIVERSAL WISDOM FOUNDATION,
INC.
#8, 3/F GILMORE I.T. CONTER BLDG.,
GILMORE AVENUE COR. FIRST
STREET, NEW MANILA, QUEZON
CITY 1112, PHILIPPINES;
TEL:632-7254375 ~77, 7226425;
FAX:632-7254908, 7215517;
Email: universal@netasia.net

SINGAPORE
AMITABHA BUDDHIST SOCIETY
(SINGAPORE), 新加坡淨宗學會
NO. 2 LORONG 35 GEYLANG
SINGAPORE 387934
TEL: 65-6744-7444; FAX: 65-6744-4774
Email: absstuas@yahoo.com

SRI LANKA
DHARMA CHAKKRA LAMA
NIVASAYA, DHARMA CHAKKRA
CHILD FOUNDATION
RERUKANA (GONAPOLA) ROAD
VEEDAGAMA BANDARAGAMA-12530,
SRI LANKA
TEL: 94-38-2291771; 94-38-2291253;
FAX: 94-38-2291253, 94-11-2508616
Email: suminda@isplanka.lk

USA
AMITABHA BUDDHIST SOCIETY OF
USA, 美國淨宗學會
650 S. BERNARDO AVE. SUNNYVALE,
CA 94087, USA
TEL: 408-7363386; FAX:408-7363389:
Email:info@amtb-usa.org ;
Website: www.amtb-usa.org

NAME OF SPONSOR
助 印 功 德 芳 名

Document Serial No : 96345

委印文號：96345

書　名：How to Live without Fear & Worry

Book Serial No.,書號：EN025

N.T.Dollars：

100,000：黃王錦鸞。

2,600：佛陀教育基金會。
The Corporate Body of the Buddha Educational Foundation

Total: N.T.Dollars 102,600 , 3,800 copies.

以上合計：新台幣：102,600 元，恭印 3,800 冊。

DEDICATION OF MERIT

May the merit and virtue
accrued from this work
adorn Amitabha Buddha's Pure Land,
repay the four great kindnesses above,
and relieve the suffering of
those on the three paths below.

May those who see or hear of these efforts
generate Bodhi-mind,
spend their lives devoted to the Buddha Dharma,
and finally be reborn together in
the Land of Ultimate Bliss.
Homage to Amita Buddha!

NAMO AMITABHA
南無阿彌陀佛

財團法人佛陀教育基金會　印贈
台北市杭州南路一段五十五號十一樓
Printed and donated for free distribution by
The Corporate Body of the Buddha Educational Foundation
11F., 55 Hang Chow South Road Sec 1, Taipei, Taiwan, R.O.C.
Tel: 886-2-23951198 , Fax: 886-2-23913415
Email: overseas@budaedu.org
Website:http://www.budaedu.org
This book is strictly for free distribution, it is not for sale.
Printed in Taiwan
3,800 copies; January 2008
EN025-7028